MONETARY, FISCAL AND TRADE POLICIES

THE DOLLAR BILL DEBATE

REPLACING NOTES WITH COINS

MONETARY, FISCAL AND TRADE POLICIES

Additional books in this series can be found on Nova's website under the Series tab.

Additional e-books in this series can be found on Nova's website under the e-book tab.

MONETARY, FISCAL AND TRADE POLICIES

THE DOLLAR BILL DEBATE

REPLACING NOTES WITH COINS

MARCUS T. ROTH
EDITOR

New York

For permission to use material from this book please contact us:
Telephone 631-231-7269; Fax 631-231-8175
Web Site: http://www.novapublishers.com

Additional color graphics may be available in the e-book version of this book.

Library of Congress Cataloging-in-Publication Data

ISBN: 978-1-62417-832-0

Published by Nova Science Publishers, Inc. † New York

CONTENTS

Preface		**vii**
Chapter 1	U.S. Coins: Benefits and Considerations for Replacing the $1 Note with a $1 Coin. Statement of Lorelei St. James, Director, Physical Infrastructure Team, Government Accountability Office. Hearing on "The Future of Money: Dollars and Sense"	**1**
Chapter 2	Statement of Beverley Lepine, Chief Operating Officer, Royal Canadian Mint. Hearing on "The Future of Money: Dollars and Sense"	**13**
Chapter 3	Statement of James C. Miller III, Former Director, Office of Management and Budget. Hearing on "The Future of Money: Dollars and Sense"	**19**
Chapter 4	Statement of Philip N. Diehl, Former Director, United States Mint. Hearing on "The Future of Money: Dollars and Sense"	**23**
Chapter 5	Statement of Richard A. Peterson, Acting Director, United States Mint. Hearing on "The Future of Money: Dollars and Sense"	**31**
Chapter 6	U.S. Coins: Alternative Scenarios Suggest Different Benefits and Losses from Replacing the $1 Note with a $1 Coin *United States Government Accountability Office*	**35**

Chapter 7 U.S. Coins:Replacing the $1 Notewith a $1 Coin Would Providea Financial Benefitto the Government **55**
United States Government Accountability Office

Index **89**

PREFACE

Since coins are more durable than notes and do not need replacement as often, many countries have replaced lower-denomination notes with coins to obtain a financial benefit, among other reasons. Six times over the past 22 years, the Government Accountability Office (GAO) has reported that replacing the $1 note with a $1 coin would provide a net benefit to the federal government of hundreds of millions of dollars annually. This book examines the net benefit to the government of replacing the $1 note with a $1 coin for the private sector and the public, and with a focus on the experiences of other countries doing so.

Chapter 1 – Statement of Lorelei St. James, Director, Physical Infrastructure Team, Government Accountability Office.

Chapter 2 – Statement of Beverley Lepine, Chief Operating Officer, Royal Canadian Mint.

Chapter 3 – Statement of James C. Miller III, former Director, Office of Management and Budget.

Chapter 4 – Statement of Philip N. Diehl, former Director, United States Mint.

Chapter 5 – Statement of Richard A. Peterson, Acting Director, United States Mint.

Chapter 6 – In March 2011, GAO reported that replacing the $1 note with a $1 coin would provide a net benefit to the government of about $5.5 billion over 30 years, or an average of about $184 million per year. This benefit, which GAO estimated using an economic model based on a set of assumptions, was entirely attributable to "seigniorage," a term defined as the difference between the cost of producing coins or notes and their face value. Seigniorage reduces government borrowing and interest costs, resulting in a financial benefit to the government. As GAO noted, the estimated net benefit could increase or decrease with changes in the assumptions.

Chapter 7 – Since coins are more durable than notes and do not need replacement as often, many nations have replaced lower-denomination notes with coins to obtain a financialbenefit. GAO has estimated the annual net benefit to the U.S. government of replacing the $1 note with a $1 coin four times over the past 20 years, most recently in April 2000. Asked to update its estimate, GAO (1) estimated the net benefit to the government ofreplacing the $1 note with a $1 coin and (2) examined other effects stakeholders suggested such a replacement could have. To perform its work, GAO constructed an economic model and interviewed officials from the Federal Reserve, the Treasury Department, the U.S. Secret Service, outside experts, and officials from Canada and the United Kingdom. To determine the effects on stakeholders, GAO interviewed officials from industries and organizations that might be affected by changes to currency.

In: The Dollar Bill Debate
Editor: Marcus T. Roth
ISBN: 978-1-62417-832-0

Chapter 1

U.S. Coins: Benefits and Considerations for Replacing the $1 Note with a $1 Coin. Statement of Lorelei St. James, Director, Physical Infrastructure Team, Government Accountability Office. Hearing on "The Future of Money: Dollars and Sense"*

Why GAO Did This Study

Since coins are more durable than notes and do not need replacement as often, many countries have replaced lower-denomination notes with coins to obtain a financial benefit, among other reasons. Six times over the past 22 years, GAO has reported that replacing the $1 note with a $1 coin would provide a net benefit to the federal government of hundreds of millions of dollars annually.

This testimony provides information on what GAO's most recent work in 2011 and 2012 found regarding (1) the net benefit to the government of replacing the $1 note with a $1 coin, (2) stakeholder views on considerations

* This is an edited, reformatted and augmented version of the testimony given on November 29, 2012 before the House Committee on Financial Services, Subcommittee on Domestic Monetary Policy and Technology.

for the private sector and the public in making such a replacement, and (3) the experiences of other countries in replacing small-denomination notes with coins. This testimony is based on previous GAO reports. To perform that work, GAO constructed an economic model to assess the net benefit to the government. GAO also interviewed officials from the Federal Reserve and Treasury Department, currency experts, officials from Canada and the United Kingdom, and representatives of U.S. industries that could be affected by currency changes.

What GAO Recommends

GAO has recommended in prior work that Congress replace the $1 note with a $1 coin. GAO continues to believe that replacing the $1 note with a coin is likely to provide a financial benefit to the federal government if the note is eliminated and negative public reaction is effectively managed through stakeholder outreach and public education.

What GAO Found

GAO reported in February 2012 that replacing $1 notes with $1 coins could potentially provide $4.4 billion in net benefits to the federal government over 30 years. The overall net benefit was due solely to increased *seigniorage* and not to reduced production costs. *Seigniorage* is the difference between the cost of producing coins or notes and their face value; it reduces government borrowing and interest costs, resulting in a financial benefit to the government. GAO's estimate takes into account processing and production changes that occurred in 2011, including the Federal Reserve's use of new equipment to determine the quality and authenticity of notes, which has increased the expected life of the note thereby reducing the costs of circulating a note over 30 years. (The $1 note is expected to last 4.7 years and the $1 coin 30 years.) Like all estimates, there are uncertainties surrounding GAO's estimate, especially since the costs of the replacement occur in the first several years and can be estimated with more certainty than the benefits, which are less certain because they occur further in the future. Moreover, changes to the inputs and assumptions GAO used in the estimate could significantly increase or decrease the results. For example, if the public relies more heavily on electronic payments in the future, the demand for cash could be lower than GAO estimated and, as a result, the net benefit would be lower.

In March 2011, GAO identified potential shorter- and longer-term costs to the private sector that could result from the replacement of the $1 note with a $1 coin. Industry stakeholders indicated that they would initially incur costs to modify equipment and add storage and that later their costs to process and transport coins would increase. However, others, such as some transit agencies, have already made the transition to accept $1 coins and would not incur such costs. In addition, for such a replacement to be successful, the $1 coin would have to be widely accepted and used by the public. Nationwide opinion polls over the last decade have indicated lack of public acceptance of the $1 coin. Efforts to increase the circulation and public acceptance of the $1 coins have not succeeded, in part, because the $1 note has remained in circulation.

Over the last 48 years, many countries, including Canada and the United Kingdom, have replaced low denomination notes with coins because of expected cost savings, among other reasons. The Canadian government, for example, saved $450 million (Canadian) over 5 years by converting to the $1 coin. Canada and the United Kingdom found that stopping production of the note combined with stakeholder outreach and public education were important to overcome public resistance, which dissipated within a few years after transitioning to the low denomination coins.

Chairman Paul, Ranking Member Clay, and Members of the Subcommittee:

I am pleased to be here today to participate in your hearing that examines the potential savings from replacing the $1 note with the $1 coin. GAO has reported six times over the last 22 years that replacing the $1 note with the $1 coin would result in net financial benefits to the government of hundreds of millions of dollars annually.[1]

In our prior reports, we recommended that Congress proceed with replacing the $1 note with the $1 coin. We continue to believe that replacing the note with a coin is likely to provide a financial benefit to the government if the note is eliminated and negative public reaction is effectively managed through stakeholder outreach and public education. However, we realize that replacing the $1 note with the $1 coin is controversial. We have previously reported on public opposition to using the $1 coin and the challenges that private businesses such as vending machine owners would face if such a transition were undertaken. Several foreign countries have already transitioned from small note denominations to coins, for a number of reasons, including the greater durability of coins and inflationary pressures.

My statement today addresses (1) our most recent estimates of the net financial benefit from replacing the $1 note with a $1 coin, (2) the long-standing public and private sector considerations of such a replacement, and (3) the experiences of other countries with replacing currency. This statement is based primarily on our most recent reports issued in March 2011 and February 2012. For our March 2011 report, to estimate the net financial benefit to the government, we constructed an economic model with data from the Federal Reserve, and the Department of the Treasury's (Treasury Department) Bureau of Engraving and Printing and the United States Mint (Mint). We interviewed government officials from Canada and the United Kingdom to obtain information about their experiences with replacing notes with coins and used the information to develop some of the assumptions used in our model. To determine the effects such a replacement would have on the public and on private business, we identified and interviewed officials from industries and organizations that could be affected by currency changes. For our February 2012 report, we updated our model to reflect actions taken by the Federal Reserve and the Treasury Department. In its most basic form, the model measures the difference between the status quo scenario— where $1 coins are available, but $1 notes predominate—and an alternative replacement scenario in which the $1 note is replaced with the $1 coin, the $1 notes are phased out, and $1 coins are produced and issued into circulation at a rate to match the way the public uses coins. Although we recognize that such a replacement would have benefits and costs for the public and for private businesses, the model was designed to estimate the net benefit and costs solely to the federal government and did not quantify the effects on the public or on private business. More detailed information on our objectives, scope, and methodology for this work can be found in the issued reports.[2] We conducted the work on which this statement is based in accordance with generally accepted government auditing standards. Those standards require that we plan and perform the audit to obtain sufficient, appropriate evidence to provide a reasonable basis for our findings and conclusions based on our audit objectives. We believe that the evidence obtained provides a reasonable basis for our findings and conclusions based on our audit objectives.

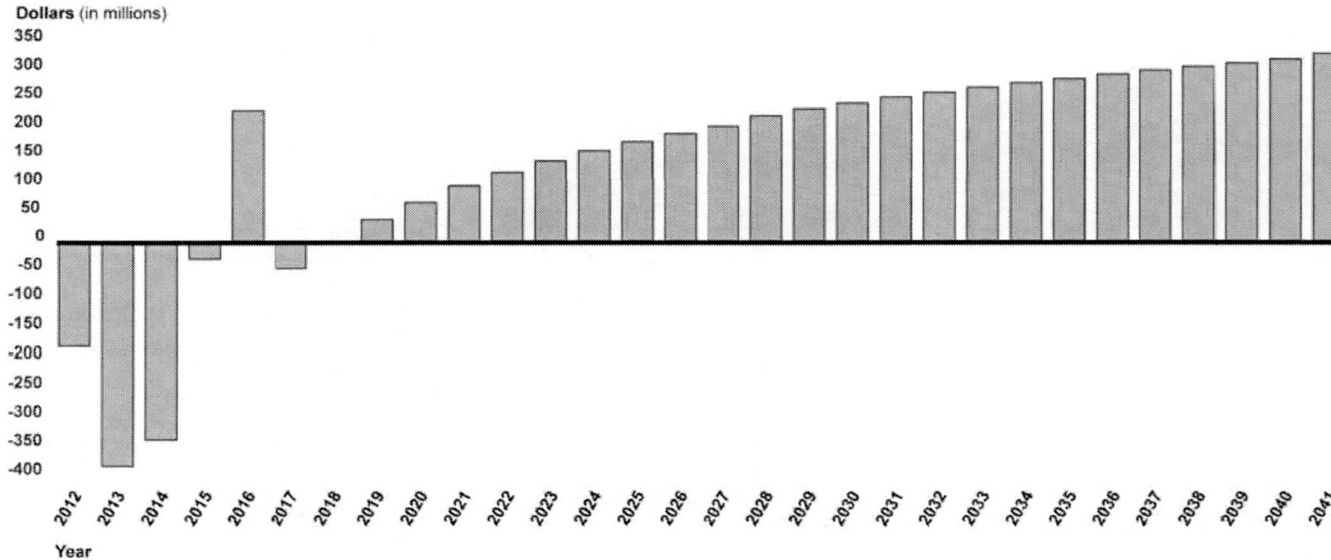

Source: GAO analysis.

Figure 1. Discounted Net Benefit to the Government of Replacing the $1 Note with a $1 Coin.

Potential Benefits from Replacing the $1 Note with the $1 Coin

In February 2012, we reported that the increased *seigniorage* resulting from replacing $1 notes with $1 coins could potentially offer $4.4 billion in net benefits to the government over 30 years. We determined that seigniorage was the sole source of the net benefits and not lower production costs due to switching to the coin, which lasts much longer than a note. *Seigniorage* is the financial gain the federal government realizes when it issues notes or coins because both forms of currency usually cost less to produce than their face value. This gain equals the difference between the face value of currency and its costs of production, which reflects a financial transfer to the federal government because it reduces the government's need to raise revenues through borrowing.[3] With less borrowing, the government pays less interest over time, resulting in a financial benefit.[4]

The replacement scenario of our 2012 estimate assumed the production of $1 notes would stop immediately followed by a 4-year transition period during which worn and unfit $1 notes would gradually be removed from circulation. Based on information provided by the Mint, we also assumed that the Mint would convert existing equipment to increase its production capability for $1 coins during the first year and that it would take 4 years for the Mint to produce enough coins to replace the currently outstanding $1 notes. Our assumptions covered a range of factors, but key among these was a replacement ratio of 1.5 coins to 1 note to take into consideration the fact that coins circulate with less frequency than notes and therefore a larger number are required in circulation. Other key assumptions included the expected rate of growth in the demand for currency over 30 years, the costs of producing and processing both coins and notes, and the differential life spans of coins and notes. We projected our analyses over 30 years to be consistent with previous GAO analyses and because that period roughly coincides with the life expectancy of the $1 coin.

As shown in figure 1, we found that the net benefit accruing each year varied considerably over the 30 years. More specifically, across the first 10 years of our 30-year analysis, replacing the $1 note with a $1 coin would result in a $531 million net loss or approximately $53 million per year in net loss to the government. The early net loss would be due in part to the up-front costs to the Mint of increasing its coin production during the transition, together with the limited interest expense the government would avoid in the first few years after replacement began.[5]

This estimate differs from our 2011 estimate, which found that replacement would result in a net benefit of about $5.5 billion over 30 years (an average of about $184 million per year) because the 2012 estimate takes into account two key actions that occurred since our 2011 report, specifically:

- In April 2011, the Federal Reserve began using new equipment to process notes, which has increased the expected life of the $1 note to an average of 56 months (or 4.7 years), according to the Federal Reserve, compared with the 40 months we used in our 2011 analysis.[6] The longer note life reduces the costs of circulating a note over 30 years and thus reduces the expected net benefits of replacing the $1 note with a $1 coin.
- In December 2011, the Treasury Department announced that it would take steps to eliminate the overproduction of dollar coins by relying on the approximately 1.4 billion $1 coins stored with the Federal Reserve as of September 30, 2011, to meet the relatively small transactional demand for dollar coins. This new policy would reduce the cost associated with producing $1 coins that we estimated in the status quo scenario and, therefore, would reduce the net benefit, which is the difference in the estimated costs between the status quo scenario and the replacement scenario.

However, like all estimates, there are uncertainties involved in developing these analyses. In particular, while the up-front costs to the Mint of increasing its coin production during the transition is reasonably certain— in large part because it is closer in time—the longer-term benefits, particularly those occurring in the later years, involve greater uncertainty because of unforeseen circumstances that could occur farther into the future. Nonetheless, looking at a longer time period allows for trends to be seen.

Moreover, changes to the inputs and assumptions used in our analysis could significantly change the estimated net benefit. For example, in 2011, we compared our status quo scenario to an alternative scenario in which the growing use of electronic payments—such as making payments with a cell phone—results in a lower demand for cash and lower net benefit. If Americans come to rely more heavily on electronic payments, the demand for cash could grow more slowly than we assumed or even decrease. By reducing the public's demand for $1 currency by 20 percent in this alternative scenario, we found that the net benefit to the government would decrease to about $3.4 billion over 30 years.[7]

In another scenario, we reported in 2012 that if interest savings because of seigniorage were not considered, a net loss of approximately $1.8 billion would accrue during the first 10 years for an average cost of $179 million per year—or $2.8 billion net loss over 30 years. While this scenario suggests that there would be no net benefits from switching to a $1 coin, we believe that the interest savings related to seigniorage, which is a result of issuing currency, cannot be set aside because the interest savings reflects a monetary benefit to the government.

Our estimates of the discounted net benefit to the government of replacing the $1 note with a $1 coin differ from the method that the Congressional Budget Office (CBO) would use to calculate the impact on the budget of the same replacement. In the mid-1990s, CBO made such an estimate and noted that its findings for government savings were lower than our estimates at that time because of key differences in the two analyses. Most important, budget scorekeeping conventions do not factor in gains in seigniorage in calculating budget deficits.[8] Thus, the interest expense avoided in future years by reducing borrowing needs, which accounts for our estimate of net benefit to the government, would not be part of a CBO budget-scoring analysis. Additionally, CBO's time horizon for analyzing the budget impact is up to 10 years—a much shorter time horizon than we use in our recent analyses.

Considerations Moving Forward

Two factors merit consideration moving forward. The first factor is the effect of a currency change on the private sector. Our 2011 and 2012 reports considered only the fiscal effect on the government. Because we found no quantitative estimates that could be evaluated or modeled, our estimate did not consider factors such as the broader societal impact of replacing the $1 note with a $1 coin or attempt to quantify the costs to the private sector. Based on our interviews with stakeholders representing a variety of cash-intensive industries, we believe that the costs and benefits to the private sector should be carefully weighed since some costs could be substantial. In 2011 we reported that stakeholders identified potential shorter- and longer-term costs that would likely result from the replacement. Specifically, shorter-term costs would be those costs involved in adapting to the transition such as modifying vending machines, cash-register drawers, and night-depository equipment to accept $1 coins. Such costs would also include the need to purchase or adapt the processing equipment that businesses may need, such as coin- counting and coin-wrapping machines. Longer-term costs would be those costs that would permanently increase the cost of doing business, such as the increased transportation and storage costs for the heavier and more voluminous coins as compared to notes, and processing costs. These costs would likely be passed on to the customer and the public at large through, for example, higher prices or fees. Most stakeholders we interviewed said, however, that they could not easily quantify the magnitude of these costs, and the majority indicated that they would need 1 to 2 years to make the transition from $1 notes to $1 coins.

In contrast to the stakeholders who said that a replacement would mean higher costs for their businesses, stakeholders from the vending machine industry and public transit said that the changeover might have only a minimal impact on them. For example, according to officials from the National Automatic Merchandising Association, an organization representing the food and refreshment vending industry, many of its members have already modified their vending machines to accept all forms of payment, including $1 coins. In addition, according to transit industry officials, the impact on the transit industry would be minimal since transit agencies that receive federal funds were required under the Presidential $1 Coin Act of 2005 to accept and distribute $1 coins.

The second factor that merits consideration is public acceptance. Our 2012 estimate assumes that the $1 coin would be widely accepted and used by the public. In 2002, we conducted a nationwide public opinion survey, and we found that the public was not using the $1 coin because people were familiar with the $1 note, the $1 coin was not widely available, and people did not want to carry more coins. However, when respondents were told that such a replacement would save the government about half a billion dollars a year (our 2000 estimate), the proportion who said they opposed elimination of the note dropped from 64 percent to 37 percent. Yet, two more recent national-survey results suggest that opposition to eliminating the $1 note persists. For example, according to a Gallup poll conducted in 2006, 79 percent of respondents were opposed to replacing $1 notes with $1 coins, and their opposition decreased only slightly, to 64 percent, when they were asked to assume that a replacement would result in half a billion dollars in government savings each year. We have noted in past reports that efforts to increase the circulation and public acceptance of the $1 coins—such as changes to the color of the $1 coin and new coin designs—have not succeeded, in part, because the $1 note has remained in circulation.[9]

Experiences of Other Countries

Over the last 48 years, Australia, Canada, France, Japan, the Netherlands, New Zealand, Norway, Russia, Spain, and the United Kingdom, among others, have replaced lower-denomination notes with coins. The rationales for replacing notes with coins cited by foreign government officials and experts include the cost savings to governments derived from lower production costs and the decline over time of the purchasing power of currency because of inflation.[10] For example, Canada replaced its $1 and $2 notes with coins in 1987 and 1996, respectively. Canadian officials determined that the conversion to the $1 coin saved the Canadian government $450 million (Canadian) between 1987 and 1991 because it no longer had to regularly replace worn out $1 notes. However, Canadian $1 notes did not last as long as $1 notes in the United States currently do.

Stopping production of the note and actions to overcome public resistance have been important in Canada and the United Kingdom as the governments transitioned from a note to a coin. While observing that the public was resistant at first, Canadian and United Kingdom officials said that with the combination of stakeholder outreach, public relations efforts, and ending production and issuance of the notes, public dissatisfaction dissipated within a few years. Canada undertook several efforts to prepare the public and businesses for the transition to the coin. For example, the Royal Canadian Mint reached out to stakeholders in the retail business community to ensure that they were aware of the scope of the change and surveyed public opinion about using coins instead of notes and the perceived impact on consumer transactions. The Canadian Mint also proactively worked with large coin usage industries, such as vending and parking enterprises, to facilitate conversion of their equipment, and conducted a public relations campaign to advise the public of the cost savings that would result from the switch. According to Canadian officials, the $1 and $2 coins were the most popular coins in circulation and were heavily used by businesses and the public. In our analysis of replacing the $1 note with a $1 coin, we assumed that the U.S. government would conduct a public awareness campaign to inform the public during the first year of the transition and assigned a value of approximately $7.8 million for that effort.

In addition, some countries have used a transition period to gradually introduce new coins or currency. For example, the United Kingdom issued the £1 coin in April 1983 and continued to simultaneously issue the £1 note until December 1984. Similarly, Canada issued the $1 coin in 1987 and ceased issuing the $1 note in 1989.

CONCLUSION

In our prior reports, we recommended that Congress proceed with replacing the $1 note with the $1 coin. We continue to believe that the government would receive a financial benefit from making the replacement. However, this finding comes with several caveats. First, the costs are immediate and certain while the benefits are further in the future and more uncertain. The uncertainty comes, in part, from the uncertainty surrounding key assumptions like the future demand for cash. Second, the benefits derive from seigniorage, a transfer from the public, and not a cost-saving change in production. Third, these are benefits to the government and not necessarily to the public at large. In fact, public opinion has consistently been opposed to the $1 coin. Keeping those caveats in mind, many other countries have successfully replaced low denomination notes with coins, even when initially faced with public opposition.

Chairman Paul, Ranking Member Clay, and members of the Subcommittee, this concludes my prepared statement. I would be pleased to answer any questions at this time.

End Notes

[1] GAO, *National Coinage Proposals: Limited Public Demand for New Dollar Coin or Elimination of Pennies*, GAO/GGD-90-88 (Washington, D.C.: May 23, 1990); GAO, *1-Dollar Coin: Reintroduction Could Save Millions If Properly Managed*, GAO/GGD-93-56 (Washington, D.C.: Mar. 11, 1993); GAO, *Dollar Coin Could Save Millions*, GAO/T-GGD-95-203 (Washington, D.C.: July 13, 1995); GAO, *Financial Impact of Issuing the New $1 Coin*, GAO/GGD-00-111R (Washington, D.C.: Apr. 7, 2000); GAO, *U.S. Coins: Replacing the $1 Note with a $1 Coin Would Provide a Financial Benefit to the Government*, GAO-11-281 (Washington, D.C.: Mar. 4, 2011); and GAO, *U.S. Coins: Alternate Scenarios Suggest Different Benefits and Losses from Replacing the $1 Note with a $1 Coin*, GAO-12-307 (Washington, D.C.: Feb. 15, 2012).

[2] GAOand GAO-12-307.

[3] Traditionally, *seigniorage* is defined as the difference between the face value of coins and their cost of production. As long as there is public demand, the government creates this net value

when it puts coins into circulation. Similarly, when the government issues notes, it creates an analogous net value, equal to the face value of the notes less their production costs. In this statement, we use the term *seigniorage* to refer to the value created from the issuance of both coins and notes.

[4] Some observers have stated that seigniorage essentially represents a tax on the public. The gains to the federal government through increased seigniorage occur because as $1 notes are replaced by $1 coins, the public will choose to hold more of their wealth in cash, thus providing a transfer to the federal government. Thus, the financial benefit to the federal government comes at a cost to the public, and there is not a net gain to society from increased seigniorage. However, this transfer occurs as a result of voluntary changes in how people are choosing to hold their wealth, which is different than in the case of a tax, which is a mandated transfer to the government.

[5] The large net benefit in 2016 would occur because we assume that the Mint's production at maximum capacity during the 4-year transition period would lead to some overproduction and thus production would drop dramatically in 2016. Because of the far lower coin production costs, the net benefit to the government would temporarily spike in that year.

[6] When notes are returned by commercial banks as deposits to the Federal Reserve, each note is processed to determine its quality and authenticity. During processing, worn and counterfeit notes are removed from circulation and the rest are wrapped for storage or re- circulation.

[7] We did not have any evidence to suggest how much demand might transfer to electronic use, but a 20 percent transfer to electronic use would appear to be a reasonably substantial change in the public's use of money. The actual number, however, could be higher or lower.

[8] *Budget scorekeeping* is the process of estimating the budgetary effects of pending and enacted legislation and comparing them with limits set in the budget resolution or legislation.

[9] GAOand GAO/GGD-00-111R.

[10] Lower-denominated currencies tend to be metal based rather than paper based because, among other reasons, these denominations tend to circulate more rapidly than higher denominations. Over time, inflation erodes the purchasing power of any particular denomination of currency. As the real value of a note declines with inflation, its more rapid circulation may wear paper notes more quickly and can make a switch to a coin cost effective.

In: The Dollar Bill Debate
Editor: Marcus T. Roth
ISBN: 978-1-62417-832-0

Chapter 2

STATEMENT OF BEVERLEY LEPINE, CHIEF OPERATING OFFICER, ROYAL CANADIAN MINT. HEARING ON "THE FUTURE OF MONEY: DOLLARS AND SENSE"*

Good afternoon. I want to thank Chairman Bachus and the respected members of this committee for inviting me to testify, on behalf of the Royal Canadian Mint, on Canada's experience with replacing the $1 bank note with a circulation coin, as well as with the introduction of an innovative coin plating technology which has dramatically improved the cost-effectiveness of circulation coins, while also improving their reliability and security.

The Mint continuously strives to improve products and services for our customers and we are quite proud of what we have achieved within our circulation coinage business, for the benefit of Canadians, as well as our international customers, since the introduction of our one-dollar circulation coin in 1987.

Although we have twice successfully managed the replacement of a low-denomination bank note with a circulation coin (with the one dollar coin in 1987 and a two-dollar coin in 1996), our record of maximizing the benefits to our circulation coins now encompasses a broad range of innovations, among them:

* This is an edited, reformatted and augmented version of the testimony given on November 29, 2012 before the House Committee on Financial Services, Subcommittee on Domestic Monetary Policy and Technology.

- Our patented **Multi-Ply Plated Steel** (MPPS) technology, first introduced on our 1-, 5-, 10- 25- and 50-cent coins in 2000 to create the most economical, durable and secure coins on the market by plating thin alternating layers of nickel and copper over a steel core -a technology used in over 70 coin denominations in 30 countries. The Mint now uses it on all Canadian circulating denominations since the launch of MPPS $1 and $2 coins in April 2012;
- Our **Alloy Recovery Program,** through which we continue to recover older alloy coins, extract their nickel content; generate revenue through bulk nickel sales; and replace the coins with new multi-ply plated product. This program has also streamlined the number of coin compositions the vending industry has to read;
- Our **Coin Recycling Program,** which allows Canadians to easily put their coins back into circulation and is a more efficient and environmentally-friendly way of supplying the market with coins by reducing the number of new coins the Mint needs to produce. Since June 2005, over six billion coins have been re circulated through this program;
- Our **High-Speed Circulation Coin Colouring** process, introduced for the first time in 2004 on a 25-cent circulation coin honouring Canadian veterans. The Mint led the industry with this technology and it continues to evolve through ever-complex applications on new commemorative circulation coins, as well as coins for international customers;
- Our new Multi-Ply Plated Steel $1 and $2 coins with **Virtual Image** and **Laser Mark** security features ideally suited to high value circulation coins;
- Our **Digital Non-Destructive Activation** (DNA) technology, by which the surface of every new $1 and $2 coin is essentially “fingerprinted” to store a unique code of that surface structure in a database. Although Canada does not have a coin counterfeiting problem, this anti-counterfeiting innovation has been proactively adopted to make our currency system even more robust, as well as to help our international customers add a potent new layer of security to their coins; and
- While a Bank of Canada Study in 2012 concluded that “cash is still the predominant payment method in terms of volume for 54°/o of transactions”, we launched our **MintChip** research and development

project to test a digital currency solution with all the features of cash, to explore the potential role of the Mint in an alternative payment world.

This highlights only a 12-year span of innovation specifically developed for the circulation coin market, but which can find application in other areas of our business, which includes collector and investment coins, and refinery operations.

While our strong focus on innovation helps the Mint compete for a greater share of the world plating market, as well as increased collector coin and bullion product sales, and fund our operations without taxpayer support, its most important outcome is our enhanced ability to meet changing customer needs while making our coinage system more robust, efficient, and reliable.

It is in this context that Canada's replacement of its one-dollar bank note with a circulation coin, and the later introduction of the two-dollar coin, can be deemed a success, from the perspective of the Mint and all end-users of Canadian currency.

Having already pointed to a number of innovations which point to the Mint's unique expertise, it is important to highlight another important and defining characteristic of our business which is the forecasting of coin inventories and the management of the coin distribution system across Canada. With distribution centres in 12 cities; 29 coin pools; and 2,000 forecasts per week, this end-to-end management of the coin supply makes us unique among the world's mints.

We also lead financial institutions and armoured car companies in managing the circulation of these coins through a network of distribution centres across Canada.

This requires timely production of Canadian circulation coins, which we consistently supply in response to market demand. By virtue of this approach, we avoid building significant inventories and prevent shortages of any denomination as we meet the fluctuating needs of Canadian trade and commerce. The prevention of coin shortages is an important performance measure for the Mint and we are proud of not having allowed any coin shortage, without building excess inventory, over the last five years.

This was an important ingredient to the success of both our past conversions from bank notes to coins, which placed a high burden of public expectation on the Mint.

Our one-dollar circulation coin was proposed by a Parliamentary committee as an outcome of public hearings in 1985 and although principally a cost-saving measure, several business and special interest groups suggested other benefits could be realized such as:

- It would be easier for transit companies to process coins than bills
- Vending machines could expand product lines and provide faster service to customers
- Organizations for the visually impaired appreciated the coin's eleven-sided, distinctive shape

Stakeholders and consumers were very receptive to this new coin. Public opinion polling revealed largely positive to neutral attitudes to the new coin and demand actually eclipsed the projected initial requirement of 250 million coins over the first three years. Instead, almost 600 million coins were produced to adequately supply the marketplace.

Canadians have come to embrace the one-dollar coin, which they nicknamed the Leonie by virtue of its iconic bird design, and use it as they would any other coin.

In a June 2012 online poll conducted on the Leonie's 25th anniversary by the CBC, Canada's public broadcaster, almost 70°/o of Canadians identified the coin as a recognizable symbol of Canada and many of those consider it a national icon equal to the beaver and maple leaf.

Despite our ability to manage production and distribution in the face of three-fold demand, our only hurdle was the continued production of the dollar bank note until 1989. This phased approach proved the only barrier to full scale adoption of the coin, which occurred soon after the last bank note was printed.

This was a lesson learned by the time Canada saw the introduction of the $2 circulation coin, which was simultaneously met by the end of two-dollar bank note production.

Lasting 25 years instead of one year for a bank note, the one-dollar circulation coin has saved the Canadian government $175 million over its first 20 years. It generated $450 million in seigniorage (the difference between the cost manufacturing and distributing a coin versus its face value, paid directly to the government) in its launch phase.

Today, the multi-ply plated steel $1 coin launched in 2012 has the same or better life, an even higher seigniorage potential and, along with the new $2 multi-ply coin, generates a combined additional $15 million annual cost savings to the government of Canada.

Since April of this year, all new Canadian circulation coinage leaving our Winnipeg, Manitoba facility is multi-ply plated steel.

Through this technology, a harmonized coinage system is minimizing costs for the Government of Canada and maximizing seigniorage revenue.

It is also widely supported by multiple stakeholders with whom the Mint worked closely and proactively to facilitate the transition from expensive, traditional alloy coins, to the most economical, durable and secure coins in the market today.

Our successful introduction of these coins depended on getting the message out early and often to all our stakeholders and in the case of the vending industry, we were able to provide first notice of this change in 2008, fully four years before the new coins started circulating this April. This allowed us to develop coins with the same look and feel as existing $1 and $2 coins despite the radical improvements they now contain.

These new coins were developed in partnership with industry and even though there were costs to operators of coin-operated equipment, our strategy of communicating early and frequently with stakeholders to facilitate the transition to new coins was widely praised.

Official statements such as that of Neil Madden, President of the Canadian Automatic Merchandising Association, summarize the merits of our initiative and its implementation:

"While no one in our industry wants to see a change that will cost us money, we do applaud the effort of our government to find cost savings. Our relationship with the Mint is strong and we value them as a partner in our industry".

Validation of our technology and implementation strategies by Canadian stakeholders is being echoed by stakeholders and customers beyond our borders.

Central banks around the world are looking for cost-effective and reliable alternatives to their expensive 100°/o alloy coins. These are customers who have much to gain from emulating the $250 million savings multi-ply plated steel has realized for the Canadian government since 2000.

We saw a pronounced shift in the international popularity of our technology when New Zealand changed all its coins to our multi-ply plated steel in 2005 and saved millions of dollars as a result of this decision. Since then, circulation coin customers on every continent are using our technology.

And as we are completing a 70,000 square foot expansion of our Winnipeg plating facility, we are looking forward to soon announcing our agreement with an Asian customer whose similar conversion to multi-ply plated steel has become the largest foreign circulation contract in our history.

I should add that industry partnerships have been very influential in the Mint's success in selling new technologies and as a case in point, our partner and licensee Jarden Zinc of Greeneville, Tennessee has been instrumental in helping us deliver multi-ply plated steel products to our international customers.

The Royal Canadian Mint is committed to advancing the science of coin engineering and manufacturing for the benefit of all its customers and stakeholders.

We are mindful of our core mandate, to support the needs of Canadian commerce by producing and distributing Canada's circulation coinage.

We have the added responsibility of managing the costs of delivering this mandate and being consistently profitable as the Mint is a self financing agency which does not does rely on any taxpayer support despite being 100% owned by the Government of Canada.

We have more than met this goal with the combined profits of the last five years eclipsing those of the previous 25. We achieved record revenues of $3.2 billion in 2011, netted profits of over $43 million and paid a record dividend of $10 million to our exclusive shareholder; the Government of Canada.

Through our many innovations, we have also found ways to improve the integrity of our coinage system with coins that incorporate better security and perform reliably. We also value the strategic relationships we have built with industry stakeholders and consumer groups to create and introduce innovations which benefit the end users of our products.

The Mint will continue to invest in research and development to keep generating solutions which meet the ever-changing needs of the marketplace and we look forward to sharing our knowledge and expertise with currency issuers all over the world looking for the best, common sense solutions to improving their coinage.

Thank you again for inviting the Royal Canadian Mint to appear before your Committee and it will be my pleasure to answer your questions.

In: The Dollar Bill Debate
Editor: Marcus T. Roth

ISBN: 978-1-62417-832-0

Chapter 3

STATEMENT OF JAMES C. MILLER III, FORMER DIRECTOR, OFFICE OF MANAGEMENT AND BUDGET. HEARING ON "THE FUTURE OF MONEY: DOLLARS AND SENSE"*

Thank you, Mr. Chairman and Members of the Committee.

It is my pleasure to speak today on a subject that I have followed for over a decade. I testified about the problems associated with eliminating the dollar bill back in 2000. The issues have changed only to the degree that substituting dollar coins for dollar bills has become an even worse deal for American businesses and consumers.

It has been quite clear from polls carried out by many sources over the years that people prefer dollar bills to dollar coins.[1] In one survey, people said the dollar bill evokes their pride in America and that eliminating it suggests erosion of our national character.[2] Americans said they see the dollar coin as a rarity, not something they use or spend. We also know they object strenuously to the elimination of the dollar bill.

Despite extensive efforts since 2007 by the Federal Reserve and financial institutions across the country to support the circulation of Presidential Dollar

---

* This is an edited, reformatted and augmented version of the testimony given on November 29, 2012 before the House Committee on Financial Services, Subcommittee on Domestic Monetary Policy and Technology.

coins, we know that more than 1.4 billion of them are stored in Federal Reserve Bank vaults – enough to satisfy the demands of commerce for the next 40 years.[3] Many of the relatively few Presidential Dollar coins issued over the past six years that are not in Federal Reserve vaults are held by consumers as collectibles or keepsakes.

As in the past, I am disturbed by allegations of huge savings from substituting dollar coins for dollar bills. If you look at various GAO reports, you find that the major portion of what they label as benefits to government stem from the interest-free loans consumers would be forced to give to government. That is, what GAO calls benefits to government are really taxes -- implicit taxes on consumers. There is no net savings here. It is a wash. Moreover, the tax is a regressive one: studies show that higher-income consumers are more likely to use alternative forms of payment such as debit or credit cards.[4] So, the tax would fall disproportionately on the poor.

Moreover, analysis of production costs for dollar notes and coins is very sensitive to assumptions. The two reports issued by the GAO in February of 2012 make it very clear that their modeling of the costs and benefits to government of substituting dollar coins for dollar bills varies enormously depending on the questions they address.[5] In fact, GAO entitled one of its reports "Alternative Scenarios Suggest Different Benefits and Losses from Replacing the $1 Note with a $1 Coin."[6] GAO stated clearly that dollar coins would always cost more to produce than dollar bills and that the purported benefits to the government come solely from seigniorage – the implicit tax on consumers. They reported that when seigniorage is eliminated from GAO's calculations, the cost to government of substituting dollar coins for dollar bills is estimated at $1.8 billion over 10 years.[7]

Even counting seigniorage, if you assume that only one dollar coin would be needed to replace each dollar bill, the government would lose $582 million over 10 years.[8] Or, if you assume, as does GAO, that it would take 1.5 dollar coins to replace each dollar bill, the government would still lose $531 million over 10 years.[9] And even with this greater seigniorage, it would take 10 years for the government to start breaking even.[10] Given the rapid development of electronic payment systems, does anyone on this Committee really think that we would be making abundant use of dollar coins 10 years from now?

The GAO has also made it clear that it has never calculated the costs to parties outside of government, including businesses and consumers. Thirteen of 15 stakeholders that it surveyed about eliminating dollar notes said they would incur both short- and long-term costs related to changing their operations to handle dollar coins.[11] It cannot be a surprise to anyone that managing coins that weigh eight times as much as notes would create significant additional handling and transportation costs. There also could be significant environmental consequences associated with transportation, but the GAO has not addressed that issue either.

The GAO tells us that if we look out over 30 years, the government would benefit from the seignioriage tax that comes from substituting three dollar coins for every two dollar bills. Why? Because coins circulate differently than bills. People leave them at home instead of recirculating them; they drop on the ground or between sofa cushions. And businesses hold onto coins longer than bills to avoid transportation costs.

So, the best that can be said for the dollar coin is that the production costs to government may be no higher than the costs of producing dollar bills. But the costs to businesses, and ultimately to consumers, are far greater. And finally, consumers would pay a huge tax that would offset precisely the government's gain on seignioriage.

In any event, it seems to me that consumers ought to be the ones making this decision. The Federal Government's sovereign power to mint money is a monopoly power, and just as a monopolist in the private sector might raise prices and stick it to consumers, a government that dictated using a means of exchange that is clearly in disfavor would be sticking it to consumers.

In conclusion, Mr. Chairman and Members of the Committee, Americans view eliminating the dollar bill as a budget gimmick, not a serious cost-cutting measure.[12] What the GAO characterizes as a benefit to the government – seignioriage -- is really a tax on the American people. The sovereign power of government to print money or to mint coins is a monopoly power, and just as monopolies impose more costs on consumers, the same thing happens when the government forecloses choices for consumers.

And finally, it seems to me that after many failed efforts to make dollar coins more appealing to consumers and the clear costs that would be shifted to them from government, the notion of eliminating the dollar bill from circulation is really quite absurd.

Thank you, Mr. Chairman and Members of the Committee: that completes my prepared statement. I shall be happy to address any questions you might have.

End Notes

[1] See, for example, GAO-11-281 (Washington, DC: March 4, 2011), p.17; GAO-03-206. (Washington DC: December 17, 2002), p. 20; and Gallup News Service, *Americans Support Dollar Coins Featuring Past Presidents* (Princeton, New Jersey: November 21, 2006).

[2] Luntz Global, October 2011.

[3] http://www.federalreserve.gov/paymentsystems/coin_data.htm#dollarcoin. See also, Board of Governors of the Federal Reserve System, *Annual Report to the Congress on the Presidential $1 Coin Program* (Washington DC: June 2012), p. 2.

[4] See, for example, Arango, Hogg, and Lee, "Why is cash (still) so entrenched? Insights from the Bank of Canada's 2009 Methods-of-Payment Survey," Bank of Canada Discussion Paper 2012-2 (Ottawa, Canada: February 2012), p. 5.

[5] GAO-12-307 (Washington DC: February 15, 2012) and GAO-12-342SP 2012 Annual Report (Washington DC: February 28, 2012). See also GAO-11-281 (Washington, DC: March 4, 2011).

[6] GAO-12-307 (Washington DC: February 15, 2012).

[7] *Ibid.*, p. 7.

[8] *Ibid.*, p. 9.

[9] *Ibid.*, p. 6.

[10] GAO-11-281 (Washington DC: March 4, 2011), p. 4.

[11] *Ibid.*, p. 19.

[12] Luntz Global, *ibid.*

In: The Dollar Bill Debate
Editor: Marcus T. Roth

ISBN: 978-1-62417-832-0

Chapter 4

STATEMENT OF PHILIP N. DIEHL, FORMER DIRECTOR, UNITED STATES MINT. HEARING ON "THE FUTURE OF MONEY: DOLLARS AND SENSE"*

Mister Chairman, Members of this Committee, it was my honor to serve as the Director of the United States Mint from 1994 to 2000. Thank you for your invitation to appear before you.

The U.S. Government Accountability Office (GAO) has, for the seventh time, gotten it right: replacing the dollar note with a dollar coin will save the United States Government and American taxpayers billions of dollars, and Congress should accept GAO's recommendation to enact this change.

GAO stands for accountability, reliability, and independence. Since 1990, GAO has issued seven reports, all reaching the same conclusion: billions will be saved. The estimated savings over 30 years have ranged from $4.4 billion to $15.7 billion. It didn't matter whether a Republican or Democrat asked the question, the answer always came back the same.

I've been gone from the U.S. Mint for 13 years, and I have no financial interest in this matter. I'm here because I think this is sound public policy. In a

---

* This is an edited, reformatted and augmented version of the testimony given on November 29, 2012 before the House Committee on Financial Services, Subcommittee on Domestic Monetary Policy and Technology.

time when Congress is considering painful cuts in government spending affecting virtually every American, why would we not take this small and painless measure. Virtually every Western economy has replaced its lowest denomination note with a coin of the same denomination, and I'll wager that no elected representative lost their job as a result. Congress has twice avoided the tough choice in passing dollar coin legislation hoping a coin could circulate alongside the dollar note despite overwhelming evidence that this will not happen.

That said, based on my own experience, I can say opponents' claims that the public will never accept a dollar coin are false. When the Sacagawea dollar coin was launched in 2000, public demand was so strong that the Mint shipped more coins in its first year, 1.3 billion, than it did in the entire 20-year history of the Susan B. Anthony dollar. Although the public greeted the Sacagawea dollar enthusiastically, the new dollar coin could not overcome the continued presence of the dollar note.

Opponents of this measure will cite survey research they claim demonstrates the public opposes substituting a dollar coin for a dollar note. But if survey respondents are informed this change will mean billions in savings, two-thirds support it.

This isn't rocket science, and no new coin is required. We did that 13 years ago. Opponents may claim the logistics are difficult or they might raise doubts about how long it will take to manufacture the 9 billion or so new coins GAO estimates will be needed to add to those already in circulation. I have doubts about these objections. During my last year as Director of the Mint we produced 28 billion coins and had capacity to produce another 2 billion that year. I understand the Mint will produce around 9 billion coins this year. Unless there has been a radical reduction in the capacity of the U.S. Mint plants in Philadelphia and Denver, and to my knowledge there has not been, the Mint is capable of meeting these requirements.

The Mint has told GAO it will need about $8 million in additional equipment, a figure that strikes me as reasonable. According to the Mint's financial reports, each dollar coin makes 82 cents in bottom-line profit for the Treasury. Spending $8 million to make $7.4 billion in net dollar coin profit sounds like a pretty good deal to me.

You have already heard all the reasons why this can't or shouldn't be done. Let me explain why I think it can, and dispel a number of the myths created to block this change.

SUCCESS THROUGHOUT THE WORLD

Considering the broad, bi-partisan support for reducing federal deficits, you would think that saving American taxpayers billions of dollars with no pain and minimal inconvenience would be welcomed. These savings aren't hypothetical- most major economies of the world, including the G-8 nations, long ago realized substantial savings from eliminating their small denomination paper currency. Canada, which made the change in 1987, reaped savings that were ten times what had been forecast. Instead of saving $175 million over 20 years, as estimated, Canadian officials later determined that they actually saved $450 million in the first five years. The change was so successful, the Canadians went for a second round, eliminating their $2 note and introducing a $2 coin in 1996.

As GAO has repeatedly stated, "Over the last 47 years, Australia, Canada, France, Japan, the Netherlands, New Zealand, Norway, Russia, Spain, and the UK, among others, have replaced lower-denomination notes with coins. Most of these replacements occurred in the 1980s."

DOLLAR COINS WORK

When I was Director of the Mint, I worked with Republicans and Democrats alike to enact the Dollar Coin Act, launching a beautiful, easily recognizable, new Sacagawea dollar coin. Today's conventional wisdom is that the dollar coin was a failure, but it certainly wasn't at the time. As I said previously, demand was much stronger than we anticipated, and we had to quickly ramp up production. In fact, demand from banks was so strong we developed a direct shipment program to reduce delivery delays through the Federal Reserve Bank (FRB).

Given some of the press reports, you might think many of those Sacagawea dollars gathered dust in (FRB) vaults. Not so. By December 2002 nearly 1.5 billion Sacagawea dollars had been issued by the Mint while only 183 million remained in FRB vaults. But demand for the new dollar coin ultimately flagged due to the loss of a champion of the coin and resistance within the government and the banking sector. Frankly, you will never overcome this resistance without removing the dollar note.

The FRB has repeatedly testified before this Committee that its vaults were bulging with unwanted dollar coins, "almost $1billion as of May 31, 2010." What you wouldn't have known without reading the fine print is that as of that same date, the FRB also held inventories of other denominations amounting to six billion coins, including 3.3 billion quarters and 1.5 billion pennies, or that coin inventory is distributed throughout a network of approximately 110 coin depots across the United States to ensure immediate availability and prevent localized shortages.

What is also noteworthy about the FRB's inventory numbers in 2010 is that new coin demand had fallen dramatically in 2009 and 2010,to an average of about 5 billion coins per year. This pattern is as regular as the night following the day. Coin demand plummets during recessions and surges with strong economic growth.

Contrast the FRB's 2009-2010 inventory with the prior four years when new coin demand averaged nearly 14 billion per year. Even with coin demand cut by 65%, the FRB still required 7 billion circulating coins in its inventory, with only one-seventh of those dollar coins.

Before the Susan B. Anthony was issued in 1979, Treasury and the Federal Reserve knew a new dollar coin could not succeed unless the dollar note was eliminated at the same time. I know because I saw the research. This knowledge was ignored. It was ignored again in 2000. I know because I was there. We need to face the simple truth: dollar coins do not circulate because we refuse to remove the dollar note.

Barriers

For many years, the dollar coin has faced another significant obstacle: the FRB's preference for the dollar note. I discovered this for myself when the Mint launched the Sacagawea dollar in 2000. The FRB is the sole channel through which the Mint distributes coins to banks and ultimately to businesses and consumers. If the FRB doesn't order a coin, it doesn't get into the hands of the public.

When we were planning the Sacagawea launch in 2000, we did an extensive survey of banks and the FRB to coordinate the logistics of distributing the new coin. They confronted us with a dilemma saying they would not order the Sacagawea dollar unless we first demonstrated there was demand for it. And they said survey research wasn't sufficient. This presented us with a Catch 22 situation since we couldn't prove there was public demand unless we could get the coin into the marketplace.

We solved this challenge by bypassing the FRB and the banks, shipping the coins directly to Wal-Mart stores nationwide. In just a few weeks, Wal-Mart distributed 100 million Sacagawea dollars as change in routine retail transactions, demonstrating that Americans welcomed the new coin. In fact, Wal-Mart wanted another 100 million coins, but when the banks started receiving calls from customers asking for the coin, they realized we had just proven public demand and they wanted shipments immediately.

This debunked another piece of conventional wisdom that Americans are opposed to eliminating the dollar note. When readily available to the public, coins are accepted. And as I said earlier, opinion polls consistently show that, when informed of the savings of substituting a dollar coin for the dollar note, two-thirds of Americans support making the switch.

Dollar coins faced other artificial barriers after the release of the Presidential Dollar coins in 2007. The FRB restricted delivery of bank orders for each new coin design to only two weeks, four times a year. What business is going to make use of a coin it isn't certain will be consistently available from its bank? This rule means businesses are unable to integrate the dollar coin into their operations so banks don't order the coin. FRB inventories then accumulate, and once again, the dollar coin is declared a failure.

SEIGNIORAGE

As GAO has reported, both notes and coins are products that make a "profit", termed "seigniorage", but they are accounted for differently. Seigniorage is the difference between the face value of a note or coin, and its cost. The FRB buys coins from the Mint *at full face value.* The Mint then records all coin seigniorage, or profit, on its books, and ultimately deposits profits into Treasury's general fund. In contrast, the FRB buys notes from the Bureau of Engraving and Printing *at cost,* with the FRB recording all note profit, or seigniorage, on its books. In 2011the FRB's note seigniorage was estimated at nearly $200 billion, and the FRB returned $77 billion to Treasury. I am not an expert on the Federal Reserve's finances, but the math here is pretty simple: eliminating the dollar note denies the FRB a significant source of its profits.

GAO Savings Estimate Likely Understated

I was surprised, as some of the Committee members may have been, by the dramatic reduction in GAO's annual savings estimate from $522 million, issued in 2000, to $184 million in its updated 2011Report. A significant part of this reduction can be attributed to the FRB's reported increase in the lifespan of the dollar note. For the past 20 years or so, the FRB had cited a lifespan of 13 to 18 months for the note. This was the case when I was Director. In 2011, the FRB more than doubled the lifespan to an average of 32 to 40 months.

Then, in preparation for the 2012 Report, the FRB provided GAO with an eye-popping lifespan estimate of 56 months, again nearly doubling the estimate from the year before. Mr. Chairman, it's hard for me to imagine what accounts for the $1note's sudden immunity to the wear and tear of circulation. Maybe we all treat the dollar bill more gently, or maybe they've developed some kind of Kevlar technology to ruggedize it. In any case, I note this change as worthy of attention.

In addition, GAO has calculated that the Mint will need four years to manufacture the quantity of dollar coins required to replace the dollar notes now in circulation and as a result the Mint will be forced to absorb dollar coin production costs without reimbursement for several years, creating a net loss during those years. As I've said, Mr. Chairman, I've been gone from the Mint for 13 years, but based on what I know of the Mint's capacity, both human and technological, I'd be very surprised if it took four years to build a sufficient inventory to replace the dollar note. My judgment is that if your legislation mandates the removal of the dollar note and gives the Mint enough time to plan for an increase in production, the Mint could produce the require inventory of coins in a year or two, with the current FRB inventory of dollar coins providing a head start. Therefore, I suggest you consider shortening the transition time, currently set at four years, so the Treasury can begin to realize these savings sooner rather than later.

Also of note, after the release of GAO's 2011Report and their estimated savings projection of $5.5 billion over 30 years, the junior Senator from Massachusetts, where the cotton-linen for the dollar note is produced, asked GAO to change its assumptions and rerun its analysis. Even with assumptions far more favorable to the dollar note, GAO still estimated savings of $4.4 billion over 30 years. Remarkably, this is the GAO analysis that opponents of this bill are criticizing, one using their chosen methodology. So if the 2012 estimate was reached through "gimmick accounting", as one opponent has said, I could venture a guess where the gimmick originated. My own opinion is that GAO's 2011estimate, without the "gimmick accounting" and changed assumptions in the 2012 estimate, is probably more sound.

CONCLUSION

Thank you, Mr. Chairman. That concludes my testimony.

In: The Dollar Bill Debate
Editor: Marcus T. Roth

ISBN: 978-1-62417-832-0

Chapter 5

STATEMENT OF RICHARD A. PETERSON, ACTING DIRECTOR, UNITED STATES MINT. HEARING ON "THE FUTURE OF MONEY: DOLLARS AND SENSE"*

Mr. Chairman, Ranking Member Clay, members of the Subcommittee, I appreciate the opportunity to appear before the Subcommittee today on behalf of the United States Mint (Mint) to address an issue that is at the top of the list of concerns of most Americans – how to save taxpayers' money. I look forward to the discussion about the Subcommittee's continued interest in the issue of $1 coins and $1 notes and cost savings regarding the manufacturing of our circulating coins.

The Mint celebrated its 220th anniversary on April 2, 2012. As one of the oldest and most visible public institutions in government, we play a special role in the life of our Nation and we have a rich history to share with the public.

The Mint is a vibrant team of 1,800 employees located in six facilities across the country. We operate three business lines: a circulating program, a

* This is an edited, reformatted and augmented version of the testimony given on November 29, 2012 before the House Committee on Financial Services, Subcommittee on Domestic Monetary Policy and Technology.

numismatic program that includes collectible products, and investment-grade precious metal bullion coins. In all business lines, the Mint had a strong performance throughout 2012. Though revenue decreased in 2012 compared to 2011, through our continued focus on costs, we were able to post solid net income results in all programs.

In 2012, the Mint made significant progress on a research and development program to examine the possible metallic alternatives for our Nation's coinage. To do so, we established and staffed a separate and secure research and development laboratory within the United States Mint at Philadelphia. This December, the Mint will provide the first annual report to Congress under the provisions of the "Coin Modernization, Oversight, and Continuity Act of 2010," which will discuss the findings of that program.

The men and women of the Mint delivered outstanding results for our Nation throughout the year. Thanks to their foresight, hard work and commitment, the Mint is well prepared for the opportunities and challenges ahead.

I would now like to discuss specific elements and highlights of the Mint's programs as they relate to today's hearing.

CIRCULATING

In fiscal year 2012, circulating coin production increased 24 percent to approximately 9.2 billion units from 7.4 billion in fiscal year 2011. Our circulating coin production has grown at a compound annual growth rate of more than 20 percent for each of the last three years since a low of 5.2 billion coins in fiscal year 2009. We are pleased with the results of the ongoing cost-reduction efforts that we began in 2009. As a result, we reduced our non-metal costs of producing circulating coins, in absolute dollars, by $58.8 million (25.5 percent) from $230.3 million in 2009 to $171.5 million as of August 2012 by improving our capacity utilization and significantly reducing expenses.

While our cost reduction efforts, increased productivity, and decreased commodity metals prices were all favorable in fiscal year 2012, the costs to manufacture and distribute both the penny and the nickel exceeded their face values again, just as they have for each of the last six fiscal years. Overall, seigniorage was positive in fiscal year 2012, and we expect it to be healthy again in 2013.

BULLION

One of our most important missions is to produce and market precious metal bullion coins to meet the needs of investors seeking exposure to silver and gold products. Although our bullion coin unit volumes and commodity prices were down in 2012, global economic and security conditions contributed to the significant volatility experienced throughout the year. In January 2012, we saw the highest monthly unit sales total in our history – with over 6.2 million ounces of bullion sold. For the fiscal year, we sold 788,000 ounces of gold bullion and 34.1 million ounces of silver bullion. Net income for the bullion program saw a decrease of 57 percent to $28.4 million from $65.8 million in 2011 because of lower volumes and pricing.

The Mint held roundtable discussions with its bullion coin Authorized Purchasers at the Philadelphia Mint in November 2011 and again last month at our facility in West Point, New York. This is the private sector network that purchases bullion coins directly from the Mint and makes them available to investors, coin and precious metal dealers, participating banks, and brokerage firms. The purpose of the meetings was to identify market trends and bullion coin demand trends. The meetings also gave us an opportunity to discuss the development and maintenance of more effective and efficient bullion coin operations and to improve communication between the Mint and the private sector.

NUMISMATIC

Results for fiscal year 2011 were exceptional for the numismatic (collector) program, with demand being driven by higher precious metal prices and the release of two popular American Eagle Silver Proof Coins. In addition, we released our most popular coin sets early in the year, increasing sales in fiscal year 2011. In fiscal year 2012, demand weakened across the board, with moderating silver prices, only one American Eagle Silver Proof Coin release, and a later-than-usual sale date for our recurring sets all contributing to a revenue decrease of approximately $241 million. We are developing a comprehensive marketing strategy to increase the numismatic customer base and to incorporate new technologies and products.

Dollar Coins

With regard to ongoing production of the $1 Coin, I want to stress that the Mint continuously looks for ways to manufacture more efficiently without compromising quality. Since 2007, the Mint has produced 2.4 billion Presidential $1 Coins. The Federal Reserve currently has approximately 1.4 billion $1 Coins in inventory. This inventory consists of Susan B. Anthony $1 Coins, Sacagawea Golden $1 Coins, Presidential $1 Coins, and Native American $1 Coins. The Mint fulfilled its statutory requirement to promote use of $1 Coins. But despite these efforts, the Federal Reserve Banks still had significant – and growing – inventories of the coins in 2011, and, as a result, production of the coins for circulation was suspended in December of last year. This suspension reduced overall Mint production expenses by $50 million. The Mint continues to offer the Presidential $1 and Native American $1 Coins through annual coin sets and other numismatic product options.

Alternative Metals

Earlier, I mentioned our progress in research and development on the possible metallic alternatives for our Nation's coinage, and I note that your second panel today will focus, in part, on the issue of minting pennies and nickels composed of steel. The Mint is looking forward to providing the first biennial report to Congress in December under the provisions of the "Coin Modernization, Oversight, and Continuity Act of 2010." At this point, I can say that we have conducted two sets of trial strikes on a variety of metallic compositions and evaluated them for attributes such as hardness, ductility, corrosion and wear resistance, electromagnetic signature, availability of raw materials, and cost. The report we submit to Congress in December will provide the results of our research and development efforts over the last 18 months. We recognize that there are many issues associated with adopting alternative metals to produce circulating coins, and we will continue to engage stakeholders in this process.

Mr. Chairman, this concludes my remarks. I will be happy to respond to any questions you or other members of the Subcommittee may have. Thank you.

In: The Dollar Bill Debate
Editor: Marcus T. Roth
ISBN: 978-1-62417-832-0

Chapter 6

U.S. COINS: ALTERNATIVE SCENARIOS SUGGEST DIFFERENT BENEFITS AND LOSSES FROM REPLACING THE $1 NOTE WITH A $1 COIN*

United States Government Accountability Office

WHY GAO DID THIS STUDY

In March 2011, GAO reported that replacing the $1 note with a $1 coin would provide a net benefit to the government of about $5.5 billion over 30 years, or an average of about $184 million per year. This benefit, which GAO estimated using an economic model based on a set of assumptions, was entirely attributable to "seigniorage," a term defined as the difference between the cost of producing coins or notes and their face value. Seigniorage reduces government borrowing and interest costs, resulting in a financial benefit to the government. As GAO noted, the estimated net benefit could increase or decrease with changes in the assumptions.

* This is an edited, reformatted and augmented version of the Highlights of GAO-12-307, a report to the Ranking Member, Subcommittee on Federal Financial Management, Government Information, Federal Services, and International Security, Committee on Homeland Security and Governmental Affairs, U.S. Senate, dated February 2012.

GAO was asked to provide additional details on its 2011 analysis. Accordingly, GAO (1) updated its analysis to account for recent changes in note processing, among other things, and based on this update determined (2) the specific benefit or loss to the government for each of the first 10 years of its 30-year analysis; (3) the net benefit or loss to the government over 10 years if the interest savings due to seigniorage are excluded from the analysis; and (4) the net benefit or loss to the government over 10 years if it is assumed that each note will be replaced by 1 coin, rather than 1.5 coins, as GAO assumed in its 30-year analysis.

GAO used the economic model it developed for its 2011 report, updated certain factors, and varied the assumptions for seigniorage and the replacement ratio of coins to notes as requested.

What GAO Found

According to GAO's updated analysis, replacing the $1 note with a $1 coin would provide a net benefit to the government of approximately $4.4 billion over 30 years, or an average of about $146 million per year. The overall net benefit was due solely to increased seigniorage and not to reduced production costs. This estimate differs from GAO's 2011 estimate because it considers recent efficiency improvements in note processing that have extended the expected life of the $1 note and other updated information. GAO's estimate covered 30 years to be consistent with previous GAO analyses and because that period roughly coincides with the life expectancy of the $1 coin.

Using the same model and assumptions used for its 30-year analysis, GAO found that replacing the $1 note with a $1 coin would provide a net loss to the government of about $531 million in the first 10 years, or an average of about $53 million per year. The cost of producing a large number of coins necessary for the transition would result in a net loss in 6 of the first 7 years. In the eighth year, and for the remaining 2 years, this situation is reversed: the interest savings outweigh the production costs and the net benefits would be positive. Overall, the net loss over 10 years compared with the net benefit GAO estimated over 30 years would occur because of large costs in the first few years to produce the initial supply of $1 coins.

If the interest savings due to increased seigniorage are excluded from the analysis, the government would incur a total net loss of about $1.8 billion over

10 years, or an average of $179 million per year. With no interest savings to offset the costs of coin production, net losses would be incurred in 9 of the 10 years. As in the preceding scenario, these production costs are greatest in the first 4 years, when a large number of coins need to be produced for the transition. Although this scenario suggests there are no net benefits of switching to a $1 coin, GAO believes that excluding the interest savings related to seigniorage omits a monetary benefit to the government.

If it is assumed that each $1 note will be replaced by 1, rather than 1.5, $1 coins, the government would incur a total net loss of about $582 million over 10 years, or an average of about $58 million per year. The costs of producing coins for the transition dominate in the first 3 years, followed by benefits in the fourth year due to the overproduction of coins during the transition. In this scenario, net losses continue to accrue through year 10. Net losses in this scenario are smaller than in the preceding scenario because fewer coins are produced and coin production costs are lower, but the one-to-one replacement does not provide increased seigniorage. Moreover, this lower replacement ratio is not consistent with the experiences of other countries that have switched from notes to coins and is likely to produce too few coins to meet demand, which could be disruptive to the economy.

In commenting on a draft of this report, the Federal Reserve and Treasury Department noted that GAO's 30-year estimate does not consider the cost to the private sector or environmental impacts. GAO agrees that such costs and impacts are important considerations, but GAO identified no quantitative estimates that could be evaluated or modeled.

February 15, 2012

The Honorable Scott P. Brown
Ranking Member
Subcommittee on Federal Financial Management,
Government Information, Federal Services, and International Security
Committee on Homeland Security and Governmental Affairs
U.S. Senate

Dear Senator Brown:

Over the past 40 years, many countries have replaced lower- denomination notes with coins as a means to provide a financial benefit to their governments.

We have reported five times over the past 22 years that replacing the $1 note with a $1 coin would provide a net benefit to the federal government of hundreds of millions of dollars annually. Most recently, in March 2011, we reported that such a replacement would result in a net benefit of about $5.5 billion over 30 years, or an average of about $184 million per year.[1] We found that this benefit was entirely attributable to an increase in seigniorage, which is the difference between the cost of producing coins or notes and their face value. To determine the estimated net benefit, we developed a model based on a set of assumptions and noted that changing these assumptions could increase or decrease the estimated net benefit. You asked us to provide additional details on our 2011 analysis and to conduct additional analyses changing two assumptions. To answer your request, we first updated our 2011 estimate because of recent changes by the Federal Reserve and Department of Treasury in note processing and $1 coin production, the results of which are provided below. We then used this updated 30-year estimate to address your request that we provide

- the specific benefit or loss to the government for each of the first 10 years for our 30-year analysis;
- the net benefit or loss to the government over 10 years if the interest savings due to seigniorage is excluded from the analysis; and
- the net benefit or loss to the government over 10 years if the replacement ratio is 1 coin to 1 note, rather than 1.5 coins for 1 note, as we assumed in our 30-year analysis.

To identify the benefit or loss of replacing the $1 note with a $1 coin, we updated the economic model developed for our 2011 report, and varied the assumptions for seigniorage and the replacement ratio of coins to notes as requested. Briefly, our model estimated net benefit or net loss to the government by subtracting the benefit of a status quo scenario from a replacement scenario. In the updated status quo scenario, notes remain the dominant form of currency at the $1 denomination, the United States Mint (the Mint) ceases production of $1 coins, the currently stored coins are gradually released into circulation to meet transactional demand, and production of $1 coins resumes after the stored coins are released.[2] In the replacement scenario, we assumed, among other things, that the production of $1 notes would stop immediately; no notes would be withdrawn from circulation, but because of their shorter life span, they would naturally fall out of circulation within a few years; the $1 coins in storage would immediately be released into circulation; and the Mint would produce a large number of $1 coins during the first 4 years of the transition. Using the updated economic model, we then varied the assumptions for seigniorage and the replacement ratio of coins to notes to determine the net benefits or losses over the first 10 years, as requested. We conducted this performance audit from November 2011 through February 2012 in accordance with generally accepted government auditing standards. Those standards require that we plan and perform the audit to obtain sufficient, appropriate evidence to provide a reasonable basis for our findings and conclusions based on our audit objectives. We believe that the evidence obtained provides a reasonable basis for our findings and conclusions based on our audit objectives.

Our Updated Estimate Shows That Replacing the $1 Note with a $1 Coin Could Provide a Net Benefit of $4.4 Billion to the Government over 30 Years

The federal government realizes a financial gain when it issues notes or coins because both forms of currency usually cost less to produce than their face value. This gain, which is known as seigniorage, equals the difference between the face value of currency and its costs of production.[3] Seigniorage reduces the government's need to raise revenues through borrowing, and with less borrowing, the government pays less interest over time, resulting in a financial benefit.

Replacing the $1 note with a $1 coin would provide a net benefit to the government of approximately $4.4 billion over 30 years, amounting to an average yearly discounted net benefit[4] of about $146 million.[5] This benefit would occur because, based on differences in how notes and coins are used in the economy, more coins than notes would have to be circulated to meet demand, and therefore more seigniorage would be created. This estimate assumes a 4-year transition period beginning in 2012, during which the production of $1 notes would stop immediately. On the basis of information provided by the Mint, we assumed that during the first year the Mint would convert existing equipment to increase its production capability for $1 coins. We also assumed that it would take 4 years for the Mint to produce enough coins to replace the currently outstanding $1 notes. Our assumptions cover a range of factors including a replacement ratio of 1.5 coins to 1 note to take into consideration the fact that coins circulate with less frequency than notes and therefore a larger number are required in circulation,[6] the expected rate of growth in the demand for currency over 30 years, the costs of producing and processing both coins notes, and the differential life spans of coins and notes. Our analyses are projected over 30 years to be consistent with previous GAO analyses and because that period roughly coincides with the life expectancy of the $1 coin.

As shown in figure 1, the annual benefit would vary over the 30 years—the government would incur a net loss in 6 of the first 7 years and then realize a net benefit in the remaining years. The early net loss would be due in part to the up-front costs to the Mint of increasing its coin production during the transition, together with the limited interest expense the government would avoid in the first few years after replacement began. The large net benefit in 2016 would occur because we assume that the Mint's production at maximum capacity during the 4-year transition period would lead to some overproduction and thus production would drop dramatically in 2016. Because of the far lower coin production costs, the net benefit to the government would temporarily spike in that year. We also found our net benefit estimate was due solely to increased seigniorage and not to reduced production costs. Like all estimates, this one is uncertain, particularly in the later years, and thus the benefit could be greater or smaller than estimated. Furthermore, inputs to our analysis, such as the costs to produce $1 notes and $1 coins, will change over time. Changes to the inputs and the assumptions used in the estimate could increase or decrease the estimated net benefit.

This estimate differs from our 2011 estimate, which found that replacement would result in a net benefit of about $5.5 billion over 30 years, or an average of about $184 million per year, because it takes into account two key actions that occurred since our 2011 report.

- In April 2011, the Federal Reserve began using new equipment to process notes, which has increased the expected life of the $1 note to an average of 56 months, according to the Federal Reserve, compared with the 40 months we used in our 2011 analysis. The longer note life reduces the costs of the status quo scenario and thus reduces the expected net benefits of replacing the $1 note with a $1 coin.

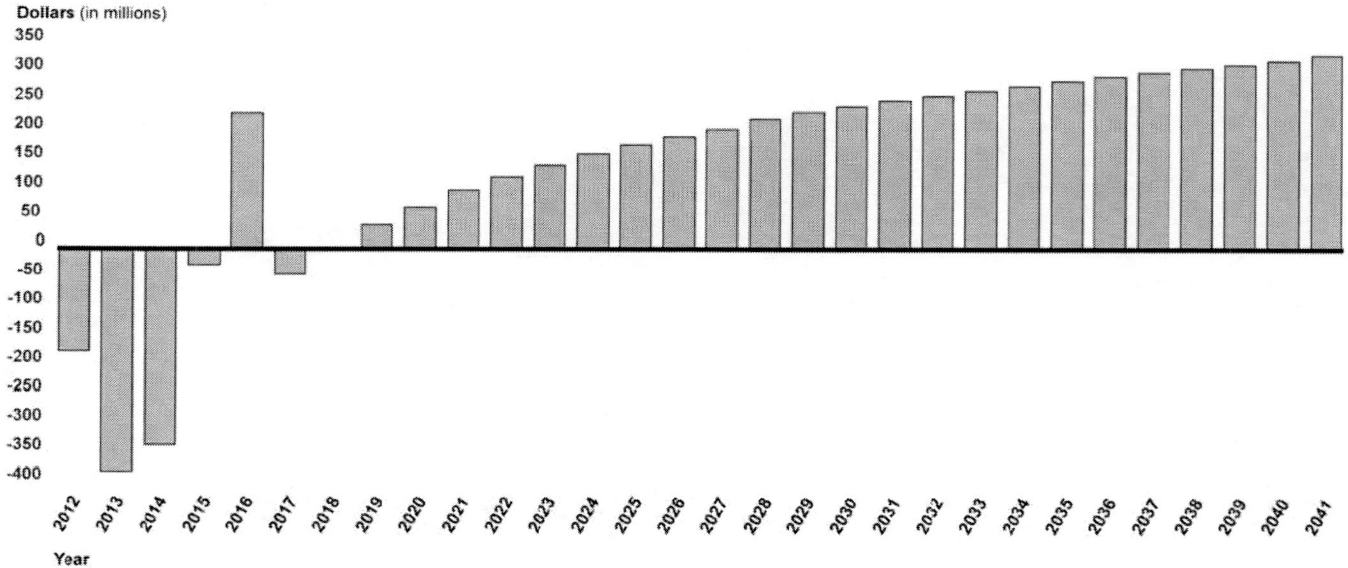

Source: GAO analysis.

Figure 1. Discounted Net Benefit to the Government of Replacing $1 Notes with $1 Coins over 30 Years, by Year.

- In December 2011, the Treasury Department announced that it would take steps to eliminate the overproduction of dollar coins by relying on the approximately 1.4 billion $1 coins stored with the Federal Reserve as of September 30, 2011, to meet the relatively small transactional demand for dollar coins. This new policy will reduce the cost of producing $1 coins that we estimated in the status quo scenario and thus reduces the expected net benefits of replacing the $1 note with a $1 coin.

In addition, our updated analysis used a start date of 2012 rather than 2011 and used the Congressional Budget Office's most recent estimates for future government borrowing costs, which are lower than the figures used in our 2011 analysis. The reduced borrowing costs reduced the net benefits of switching to a $1 coin.[7]

Finally, as in our 2011 report, we considered only the fiscal effect of this change on the government. We did not consider other factors, such as the relative environmental and societal costs and benefits of the status quo and a replacement. Further analysis would be needed to determine, for example, whether the net effects of a replacement would be positive or negative for the environment,[8] or how the costs to industry would compare with the net benefit to the government. As we noted in our 2011 report, the costs to industry of a replacement are difficult to quantify and, according to stakeholders we spoke to, would include both near-term transition costs, such as the costs of retooling cash drawers, and longer- term costs from structural changes to ways of doing business, such as higher transportation costs incurred by armored carriers since coins are heavier than notes.

Replacing the $1 Note with a $1 Coin Would Result in a $531 Million Net Loss over the First 10 Years

Across the first 10 years of our 30-year analysis, replacing the $1 note with a $1 coin would result in $531 million in net loss, or approximately $53 million per year in net loss to the government. For this analysis, we maintained all the key assumptions of our 30-year analysis—notably that 1.5 coins would be produced to replace each $1 note and that the demand for $1-denominated currency continues to grow each year. As shown in figure 2, the cost of producing coins would result in a net loss in 6 of the first 7 years when the Mint produced $1 coins at high levels to enable the transition. Net benefits would occur in each of the remaining years. Overall, the net loss over the first 10 years compared with the benefits we estimated over 30 years would occur because of large costs during the first 4 years to produce the initial supply of $1 coins, while the benefits of reduced interest expense due to increased seigniorage would occur more heavily in later years.

WITHOUT COUNTING SEIGNIORAGE, SWITCHING TO A $1 COIN WOULD RESULT IN A NET LOSS

Under a scenario that does not consider interest savings due to seigniorage, a net loss of approximately $1.8 billion would accrue during the 10-year period for an average cost of $179 million per year. As shown in figure 3, net losses would be incurred in 9 of the 10 years. In particular, large costs would be incurred in each of the first 4 years because of the large number of coins that would need to be produced for the transition, as was the case in the scenario discussed above. As in the previous analysis, in year 5, there would be a temporary net benefit because coins would be overproduced during the previous 4 years and coin production would fall to zero in that year—and the cost is therefore less than the cost of producing $1 notes that would have been incurred had the transition not taken place. After year 5, net losses would continue to be incurred because, although the life of a $1 coin is longer than the life of a $1 note, coins cost more than notes to produce. All of the scenarios assume that additional currency would need to be produced not only to replace worn out or lost currency, but also to support a growing economy. Thus, in this scenario, we found that even with the longer life of the $1 coin, the cost of producing coins for the growing economy after the transition would exceed the cost of producing $1 notes in each of those years that would have been incurred without the replacement. While this scenario suggests that there would be no net benefits from switching to a $1 coin, we believe that not including the interest savings related to seigniorage omits a monetary benefit to the government.

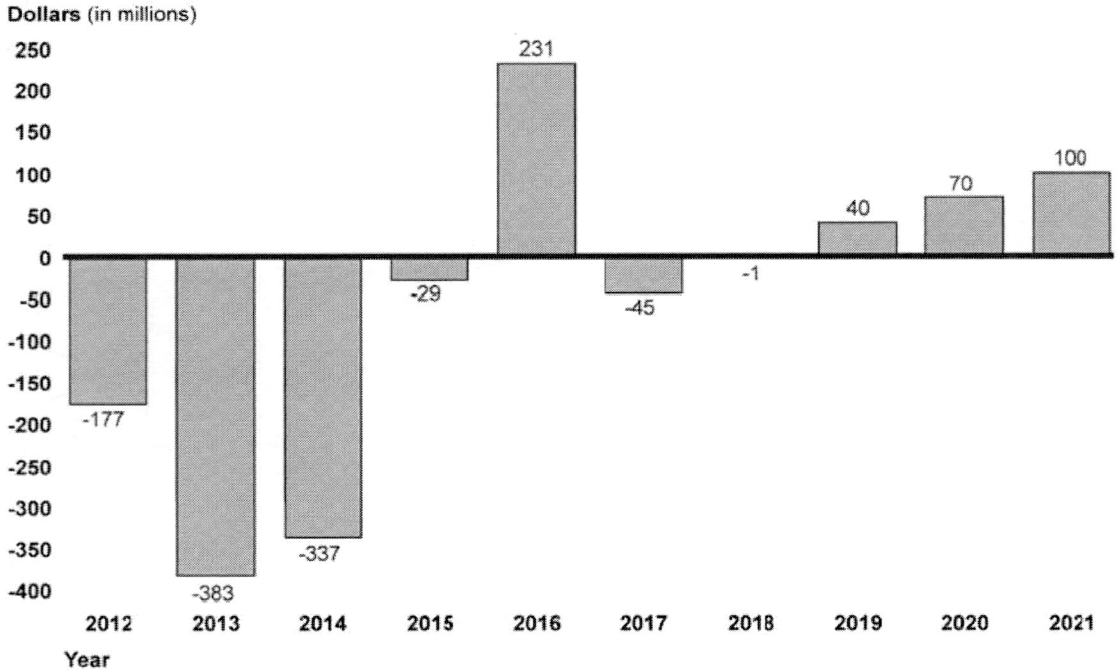

Source: GAO analysis.

Note: The large net benefit in 2016 occurs because we assume that the Mint's production at maximum capacity during the 4-year transition period will lead to some overproduction and production drops dramatically in 2016. Because of the far lower coin production costs, the net benefit to the government will temporarily spike in that year.

Figure 2. Net Benefits and Net Losses to the Government over the First 10 Years.

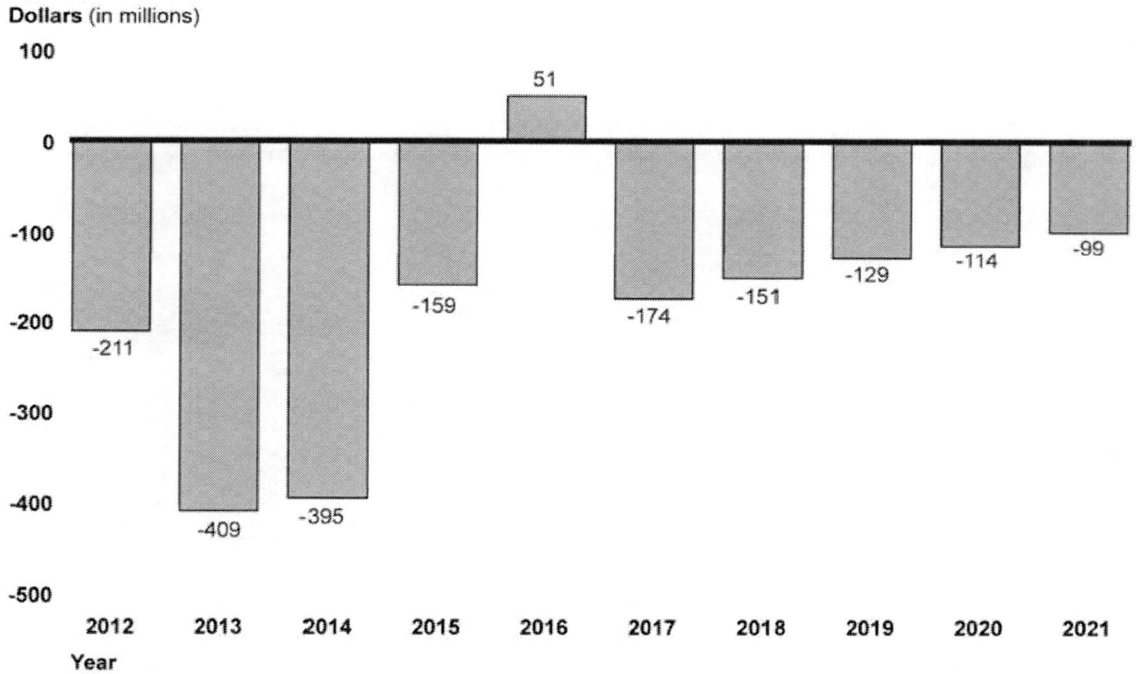

Source: GAO analysis.

Note: The net benefit in 2016 occurs because we assume that the Mint's production at maximum capacity during the 4-year transition period will lead to some overproduction and production drops dramatically in 2016. Because of the far lower coin production costs, the net benefit to the government will temporarily spike in that year.

Figure 3. Net Benefits and Net Losses to the Government Excluding Seigniorage.

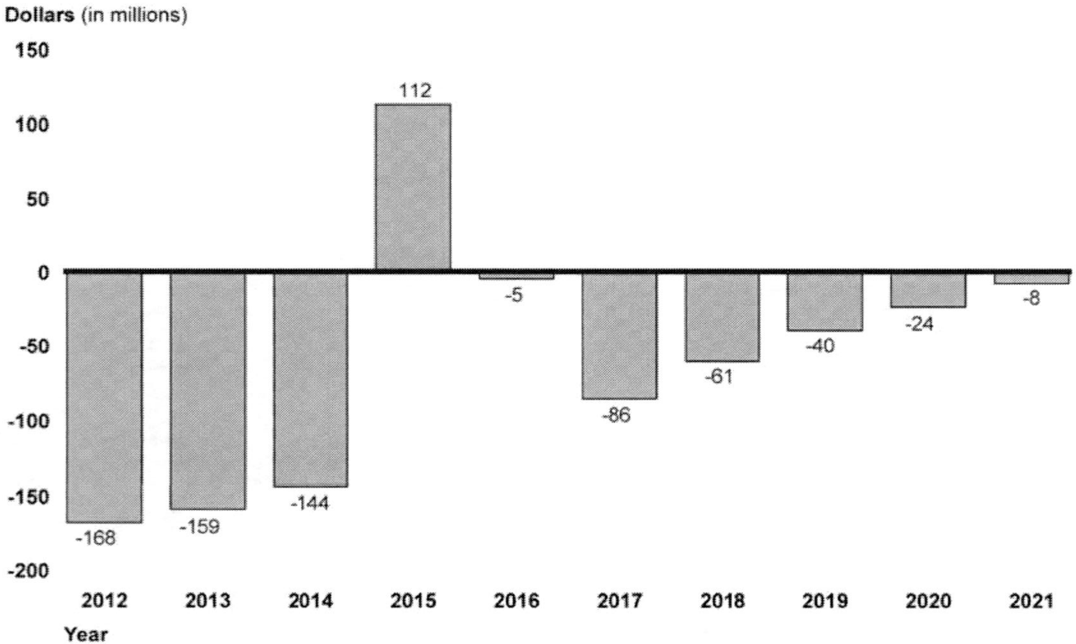

Source: GAO analysis.

Note: The large net benefit in 2015 occurs because we assume that the Mint's production at maximum capacity during the transition period will lead to some overproduction and production drops dramatically in 2015. Because of the far lower number of coins produced in a one coin to one note replacement scenario and the corresponding lower production costs, the net benefit to the government will temporarily spike 1 year earlier than in the other scenarios.

Figure 4. Net Benefits and Net Losses to the Government Assuming a 1-to-1 Replacement Ratio.

SWITCHING TO A $1 COIN WOULD RESULT IN A NET LOSS IF COINS REPLACED NOTES ON A 1-TO-1 BASIS

Under this scenario, we include the net benefits of interest savings related to seigniorage, but assume that a single $1 coin would be produced to replace each $1 note. In total, across the 10 years the total net loss of switching to $1 coins would be $582 million, or just over $58 million per year. As shown in figure 4, net losses would be incurred in 9 of 10 years of this scenario. The costs of producing coins for the transition are highest in the first 3 years, followed by benefits in the fourth year because of the overproduction of coins during the transition. In this scenario, net losses would continue through year 10.

In this scenario, far fewer coins would be produced because of the low replacement ratio, and thus the costs associated with their production would be much less than in the previous scenarios. However, this scenario also involves no gains to the government because of seigniorage because only one coin would be produced to replace each note that will fall out of circulation. In fact, the replacement case in this scenario results in reduced seigniorage relative to the status quo because the cost of producing a note is less than the cost of producing a coin, so each $1 coin has less seigniorage associated with its issuance than the $1 note it is replacing.

A caution concerning a 1-to-1 replacement of coins to notes is that under this scenario, there would likely not be enough coins to meet demand. A shortage of currency could have significant negative consequences for the economy, such as hampering cash transactions. As we noted in our 2011 report, other countries that have switched from notes to coins have found that, because people use notes and coins differently, the number of coins needed for a replacement is greater than the number of notes to be replaced. While the actual replacement ratio needed is not known ahead of any transition, our 2011 analysis of the transition to a $1 coin in Canada and the £1 coin in the United Kingdom led us to decide that a 1.5-to-1 ratio was a reasonable level.

CONCLUDING OBSERVATIONS

Estimating whether the government would derive benefits from replacing the $1 note with a $1 coin requires an analysis with many assumptions. As is clear from the findings in this report, not accounting for the benefits related to increased seigniorage can substantially affect the estimate. While we identified and updated a few factors used in these analyses that changed since our 2011 report, other factors could also change over time, such as the cost of inputs for notes and coins or changes in the use of cash by the public, among other things. As such, these analyses are highly affected by changing conditions as well as by conceptual views on certain key issues, such as seigniorage and replacement ratios.

AGENCY COMMENTS AND OUR EVALUATION

We provided a draft of this report to the Federal Reserve and the Department of the Treasury for review and comment. Their written comments are reprinted in appendixes I and II, respectively. The Federal Reserve noted that it believes our 30-year estimate may overstate the net financial benefit to the government because it (1) does not adequately address the costs to the private sector, state and local government, and the Federal Reserve and (2) does not consider potential increases in the cost of raw material for coins or possible future changes in discount rates. Similarly, the Treasury Department noted that our analysis should consider the cost to the private sector and the impact on the environment. We agree that the benefits and costs to the private sector and the impact on the environment are important considerations. However, we found no quantitative estimates of the costs to the private sector or environmental impacts that could be evaluated or modeled. We did not assess potential environmental impacts because these concerns were beyond the scope of our analysis and we did not identify quantitative estimates of such impacts. We included all relevant costs to the Federal Reserve that the agency provided to us and found no data on the cost to state and local governments. We used the best data available on coin production costs, which accounts for the cost of raw materials, and we used the most current discount rate. Furthermore, we recognize that our analyses are highly affected by changing conditions, such as changes in the cost of coins and notes, which may alter the total cost savings associated with replacing the $1 note with a $1 coin.

In addition, the Federal Reserve noted an increased risk of counterfeiting associated with replacing the $1 note with a $1 coin. We reported in 2011 that counterfeiting of U.S. coins is currently minimal, according to the U.S. Secret Service.[9] The Federal Reserve also noted that we did not provide a sensitivity analysis that varies key assumptions such as possible increases in the public's use of electronic payments. In 2011, we reported the results of our sensitivity analyses, including one in which replacement leads to a decrease in the demand for currency as people switch to electronic payments. The Treasury also provided technical comments, which we addressed as appropriate.

We are sending copies of this report to the appropriate congressional committees, the Secretary of the Treasury, and the Chairman of the Federal Reserve. The report will also be available at no charge on the GAO Web site at http://www.gao.gov.

If you or your staff have any questions about this report, please contact me at (202) 512-2834 or by e-mail at stjamesl@gao.gov. Contact points for our Offices of Congressional Relations and Public Affairs may be found on the last page of this report. GAO staff that made key contributions to this report include Teresa Spisak (Assistant Director), Amy Abramowitz, Lindsay Bach, Patrick Dudley, Bess Eisenstadt, and David Hooper.

Sincerely yours,
Lorelei St. James
Director, Physical Infrastructure Issues

APPENDIX I. COMMENTS FROM THE BOARD OF GOVERNORS OF THE FEDERAL RESERVE SYSTEM

BOARD OF GOVERNORS
OF THE
FEDERAL RESERVE SYSTEM
WASHINGTON, D.C. 20551

JEFFREY C. MARQUARDT
DEPUTY DIRECTOR
DIVISION OF
RESERVE BANK OPERATIONS
AND PAYMENT SYSTEMS

February 9, 2012

Ms. Lorelei St. James
Director
Physical Infrastructure Issues
U.S. Government Accountability Office
441 G Street, N.W.
Washington, D.C. 20548

Dear Ms. St. James:

Thank you for the opportunity to comment on the GAO's draft report "Alternative Scenarios Suggest Different Benefits and Losses from Replacing the $1 Note with a $1 Coin." Under the alternative scenarios analyzed by the GAO in this report (limiting the analysis to 10 years, excluding seigniorage, and reducing the number of coins needed to replace each note from 1.5 to 1) the government would experience losses of between $531 million and $1.8 billion over the first 10 years of the program. The GAO projects a financial benefit to the government of about $4.4 billion over 30 years; we are concerned that the 30-year savings projection may overstate the net financial benefit to the government, perhaps substantially.

Overall, the report states that the cost of producing sufficient coins to replace all $1 notes is never fully recovered during the 30-year analysis; all savings are attributable to increased seigniorage income.[1] In fact, there is no year in the study in which estimated non-seigniorage benefits exceed costs. Moreover, the analysis does not adequately address the costs to the Federal Reserve of such a replacement and does not address at all the broader societal costs to consumers, retailers and other businesses, and state and local governments.

The analysis also does not address the counterfeiting risks associated with replacing the $1 note with a $1 coin. The current low rate of counterfeiting helps maintain global confidence in U.S. currency. Unlike the $1 note, the $1 coin does not have any effective machine-readable or publicly-usable counterfeit deterrent features. Several countries that have converted low denomination notes to coins have reported higher levels of counterfeiting for low-denomination coins than previously observed for low-denomination notes, and the U.S. Sacagawea $1 coin was counterfeited in some Latin American countries soon after the U.S. Mint issued it.

[1] The Congressional Budget Office does not score seigniorage in its budget calculations.

Finally, the GAO did not provide a sensitivity analysis that reflects some possibly significant risks to its assumptions, such as possible changes in the public's means of making payments over the decades in which seigniorage benefits are highest. Although the value of Federal Reserve notes in circulation increased more than 7 percent annually over the past several years, the growth rate for $1 notes has been on average only 2 percent per year. It is possible that the elimination of the $1 note could accelerate the ongoing shift of consumer payments to debit cards and other electronic payment alternatives. In addition to potential shifts in consumer payment methods, the analysis did not consider potential increases in raw material costs for coins, or changes in discount rates. Given the near-term expenses associated with the transition and uncertainty of the long-term forecasted benefits, it is possible that no savings will ever be realized from the replacement of $1 notes with $1 coins. Sensitivity analysis for these factors would help provide a greater confidence level around long-term savings projections, which are highly dependent on discount rate and other assumptions. In fact, changes in assumptions have reduced the GAO's 30-year average annual net benefit projections from $550 million in its 2000 study, to $186 million in its 2011 study, to $146 million in the 2012 Duplication and Cost Savings report; in this study, 10-year average annual net costs to the government ranged from $53 million to $179 million.

Proponents of replacing $1 notes with $1 coins often cite similar steps that have been taken in other economies in recent decades as an indication that such a change has strong financial benefits. In general, the low-denomination note that was replaced in those economies had a far shorter useful life (typically three to six months) than is the case with the $1 note, which currently has a useful life of about 56 months. Further, these decisions were typically made when electronic payment substitutes for cash were less mature than in the current U.S. environment. Therefore, the decisions of other economies have been based on very different circumstances than exist in the United States.

We continue to believe that a fuller societal cost-benefit analysis and a sensitivity analysis that varies key assumptions that are subject to material uncertainty would provide policy-makers with a more complete basis for considering the future of the $1 note and $1 coin.

Sincerely,

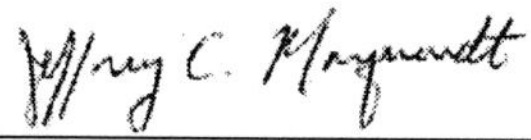

Appendix II. Comments from the Department of the Treasury

DEPARTMENT OF THE TREASURY
WASHINGTON, D.C.

1789

ASSISTANT SECRETARY

February 10, 2012

Ms. Teresa Spisak
Assistant Director, Physical Infrastructure
Government Accountability Office
441 G Street, NW
Washington, DC 20548

Dear Ms. Spisak:

Thank you for the opportunity to review and comment on the Government Accountability Office (GAO) draft report, "*Alternative Scenarios Suggest Different Benefits and Losses from Replacing the $1 Note with a $1 Coin*" (GAO-12-307R).

We have reviewed the draft report, which updates an analysis GAO performed last year. As you know, the Department of the Treasury has not taken a position on whether the $1 note should be replaced by the $1 coin. We welcome the GAO's analysis as Congress continues to consider this issue and have the following comments:

First, as we noted in our response to the GAO's report on this subject, the GAO has not considered the total cost associated with replacing the $1 note with the $1 coin, including transportation, production, environmental, and other costs. In our view, policymakers should consider both the direct financial benefit to the Government *and* the cost impact on the private sector and the environment.

Second, as your draft report notes, in December 2011, Secretary Geithner ordered the suspension of production of new Presidential $1 coins for circulation. There is very limited transactional demand for $1 coins so long as the $1 note and $1 coin co-circulate. A supply of more than 1.4 billion surplus $1 coins had built up in the vaults of Federal Reserve Banks – enough to meet current levels of circulating demand for more than a decade. In light of this, Treasury sought to reduce taxpayer costs by eliminating the unnecessary production of additional surplus $1 coins. Regular circulating demand will be met through the Federal Reserve Banks' existing inventory of nearly 1.4 billion $1 coins, which will be drawn down over time. We estimate that this action will save taxpayers at least $50 million annually. If Congress decided to eliminate the $1 note and replace it with the $1 coin, however, then the demand for dollar coins would increase and the Secretary would direct the United States Mint to produce enough dollar coins to meet the demand.

Again, thank you for the opportunity to review and comment on this draft report. Technical comments are provided for your consideration under separate cover.

Sincerely,

Dan Tangherlini
Assistant Secretary for Management
and Chief Financial Officer

GAO's Mission

The Government Accountability Office, the audit, evaluation, and investigative arm of Congress, exists to support Congress in meeting its constitutional responsibilities and to help improve the performance and accountability of the federal government for the American people. GAO examines the use of public funds; evaluates federal programs and policies; and provides analyses, recommendations, and other assistance to help Congress make informed oversight, policy, and funding decisions. GAO's commitment to good government is reflected in its core values of accountability, integrity, and reliability.

End Notes

[1] GAO, *U.S. Coins: Replacing the $1 Note with a $1 Coin Would Provide a Financial Benefit to the Government*, GAO-11-281 (Washington, D.C.: Mar. 4, 2011).

[2] As of September 30, 2011, approximately 1.4 billion $1 coins were stored with the Federal Reserve.

[3] Traditionally, seigniorage is defined as the difference between the face value of coins and their cost of production. As long as there is public demand, the government creates this net value when it puts coins into circulation. Similarly, when the government issues notes, it creates an analogous net value, equal to the face value of the notes less their production costs. In this report, we use the term "seigniorage" to refer to the value created from the issuance of both coins and notes.

[4] A discounted net value uses a rate, known as the discount rate, to convert the value of payment or receipts expected in future years to today's value, taking into account that the further into the future an amount is paid or received, the smaller its value is today. Applying a discount rate establishes a consistent basis for comparing alternative investments that will have differing patterns of costs and benefits over many years.

[5] Our estimate of the discounted net benefit to the government of replacing the $1 note with a $1 coin is not intended to replicate budget scoring that would be conducted by the Congressional Budget Office.

[6] As explained in more detail later, we used a 1.5-to-1 replacement ratio based on our analysis of the experiences of Canada and the United Kingdom.

[7] In addition to the changes listed above, we revised the level of transactional demand for coins that is assumed to exist in the status quo scenario. On the basis of updated information from the Federal Reserve, we assumed a smaller transactional demand for coins. This change had only a minimal impact on the findings.

[8] For example, officials from the Bureau of Printing and Engraving pointed out that replacing the $1 note with a $1 coin would also have environmental impacts relating to obtaining raw materials and carbon dioxide emissions, among others.

[9] GAO-11-281.

In: The Dollar Bill Debate
Editor: Marcus T. Roth

ISBN: 978-1-62417-832-0

Chapter 7

U.S. COINS:REPLACING THE $1 NOTEWITH A $1 COIN WOULD PROVIDEA FINANCIAL BENEFITTO THE GOVERNMENT*

United States Government Accountability Office

ABBREVIATIONS

BEP	Bureau of Engraving and Printing
CBO	Congressional Budget Office
Mint	United States Mint
Treasury	Department of the Treasury
UK	United Kingdom

WHY GAO DID THIS STUDY

Since coins are more durable than notes and do not need replacement as often, many nations have replaced lower-denomination notes with coins to obtain a financialbenefit. GAO has estimated the annual net benefit to the U.S.

* This is an edited, reformatted and augmented version of the United States Government Accountability Officereport to Congressional Requesters publication GAO-11-281, dated March, 2011.

government of replacing the $1 note with a $1 coin four times over the past 20 years, most recently in April 2000. Asked to update its estimate, GAO (1) estimated the net benefit to the government ofreplacing the $1 note with a $1 coin and (2) examined other effects stakeholders suggested such a replacement could have. To perform its work, GAO constructed an economic model and interviewed officials from the Federal Reserve, the Treasury Department, the U.S. Secret Service, outside experts, and officials from Canada and the United Kingdom. To determine the effects on stakeholders, GAO interviewed officials from industries and organizations that might be affected by changes to currency.

What GAO Recommends

As in the past, GAO's analysis indicates that replacing the $1 note with a $1 coin would provide a financial benefit to the government if production of the $1 note ceased. GAO previously recommended replacement of the $1 note and continues to support this recommendation. The Federal Reserve and Treasury reviewed a draft of this report and both noted the importance of societal effects in deciding on such a replacement and offered technical comments.

What GAO Found

According to GAO's analysis, replacing the $1 note with a $1 coin could save the government approximately $5.5 billion over 30 years. This would amount to an average yearly discounted net benefit—that is, the present value of future net benefits—of about $184 million. However, GAO's analysis, which assumes a 4-year transition period beginning in 2011, indicates that the benefit would vary over the 30 years. As shown in the figure below, the government would incur a net loss in the first 4 years and then realize a net benefit in the remaining years. The early net loss is due in part to the up-front costs to the U.S. Mint of increasing its coin production during the transition. GAO's current estimate is lower than its 2000 estimate, which indicated an annual net benefit to the government of $522 million. This is because some information has changed over time and GAO incorporated some different assumptions in its economic model.

For example, the lifespan of the note has increased over the past decade, and GAO assumed a lower ratio of coins to notes needed for replacement. GAO has noted in past reports that efforts to increase the circulation and public acceptance of the $1 coin have not succeeded, in part, because the $1 note has remained in circulation. Other countries that have replaced a low-denomination note with a coin, such as Canada and the United Kingdom, stopped producing the note. Officials from both countries told GAO that this step was essential to the success of their transition and that, with no alternative to the note, public resistance dissipated within a few years.

Stakeholders representing a variety of cash-intensive entities in the private sector identified potential shorter- and longer-term effects of a replacement. For example, some stakeholders said that they would initially incur costs to modify equipment and add storage and that later their costs to process and transport coins would go up. Others, however, such as some transit agencies, have already made the transition and would not incursuch initial costs.

Discounted Net Benefits by Year Resulting from Replacing the $1 Note with a $1 Coin

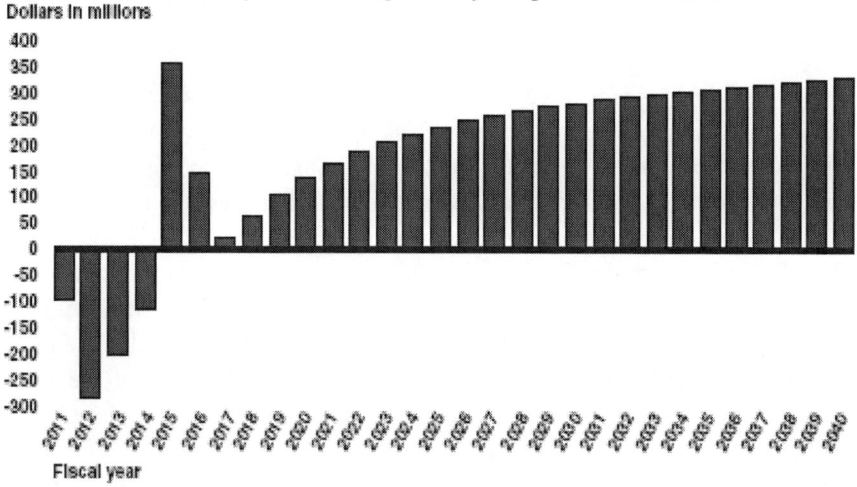

Source: GAO analysis.

March 4, 2011

The Honorable Richard C. Shelby
Ranking Member
Committee on Banking, Housing
and Urban Affairs United States Senate

The Honorable Robert P. Casey
United States Senate

The Honorable Tom Harkin
United States Senate

Over the past 40 years, many countries have replaced lower-denomination notes with coins as a means of providing a financial benefit to their governments. We have reported four times over the past 20 years that replacing the $1 note with a $1 coin would provide a net benefit to the government of hundreds of millions of dollars annually.[1] Most recently, in 2000, we estimated a net benefit to the government of about $522 million annually.[2] Because this last estimate was a decade old, you asked us to update it and describe some potential effects of replacing the $1 note with a $1 coin. To accomplish these objectives, we addressed the following questions: (1) What is the estimated net benefit, if any, to the government of replacing the $1 note with a $1 coin? (2) What other effects did stakeholders suggest such a replacement could have?

To estimate the net benefit to the government of replacing the $1 note with a $1 coin, we constructed an economic model with data from the Board of Governors of the Federal Reserve System (Federal Reserve), the Bureau of Engraving and Printing (BEP), and the United States Mint (Mint). We analyzed past GAO and Federal Reserve reports that previously estimated the net benefit to the government of such a replacement. We interviewed officials from two bureaus of the Department of the Treasury (Treasury)— BEP and the Mint—the Federal Reserve, and the Department of Homeland Security's U.S. Secret Service to develop the structure, inputs, and assumptions for the model. In addition, we interviewed government officials in Canada and the United Kingdom (UK) to obtain information about their experiences replacing notes with coins and used this information to develop some of the model assumptions. To determine the effects such a replacement could have, we identified industries and organizations that might be affected by changes to currency. We interviewed private entities involved in the production of materials for and processing of notes and coins; 15 associations and companies that represent five major industries that often deal in cash—banking and financial institutions; grocery and convenience stores; and vending, transit, and retail businesses. We conducted this performance audit from June 2010 to March 2011 in accordance with generally accepted government auditing standards. These standards require that we plan and perform the audit to obtain sufficient, appropriate evidence to provide a reasonable basis for our findings and conclusions based on our audit objectives. We believe that the evidence obtained provides a reasonable basis for our findings and conclusions based on our audit objectives. Appendix I contains more detailed information on our scope and methodology.

BACKGROUND

To promote efficient commercial exchange and economic growth, national governments and central banks issue money, including paper notes and coins in various denominations. The federal government experiences a financial gain when it issues notes or coins because both forms of currency usually cost less to produce than their face values. As long as there is a public demand, when the government puts coins into circulation, it creates a value known as "seigniorage." Seigniorage is traditionally defined as the difference between the face value of coins and their cost of production. In addition, the face value of notes issued, net of their production costs, creates an analogous net value for the federal government. In this report, we use the term "seigniorage" to refer to the value created from the issuance of both coins and notes. Seigniorage reduces the government's need to raise other revenues, thus reducing the amount of money that the government needs to borrow.[3] When the government has to borrow less, it pays less in interest over time. Although the interest avoided is a benefit to the government, the public effectively finances this benefit by choosing to hold more cash on which it does not earn interest.

Two Treasury bureaus, BEP and the Mint, produce notes and coins, respectively, and the Federal Reserve places them in circulation through banks in response to public demand. Under current law, the Federal Reserve determines the amount of $1 notes necessary for commerce.[4] For the circulation of $1 coins, the Secretary of the Treasury decides what is necessary to meet the needs of the United States.[5] In practice, according to officials from the Mint and the Federal Reserve, the Federal Reserve makes this determination by producing a short-term forecast of demand for notes and coins. Based on this forecast, the Federal Reserve orders notes from BEP and the 12 regional Federal Reserve banks order coins from the Mint. The Federal Reserve circulates the notes through the Federal Reserve banks and the Mint distributes coins directly to those banks. The Federal Reserve banks distribute notes and coins to commercial banks to meet the demand of retailers and the public. When notes and coins are returned by commercial banks as deposits to the Federal Reserve banks, each note is processed to determine its quality and authenticity. During processing, worn and counterfeit notes are removed from circulation and the rest are wrapped for storage or re-circulation. While the Federal Reserve re-circulates coins received from banks, it does not have a comparable program to test the authenticity or fitness of coins. The Federal Reserve contracts with private entities such as armored carriers to count, sort, and transport notes and coins for circulation or storage. Figure 1 shows the production and circulation of notes and coins.

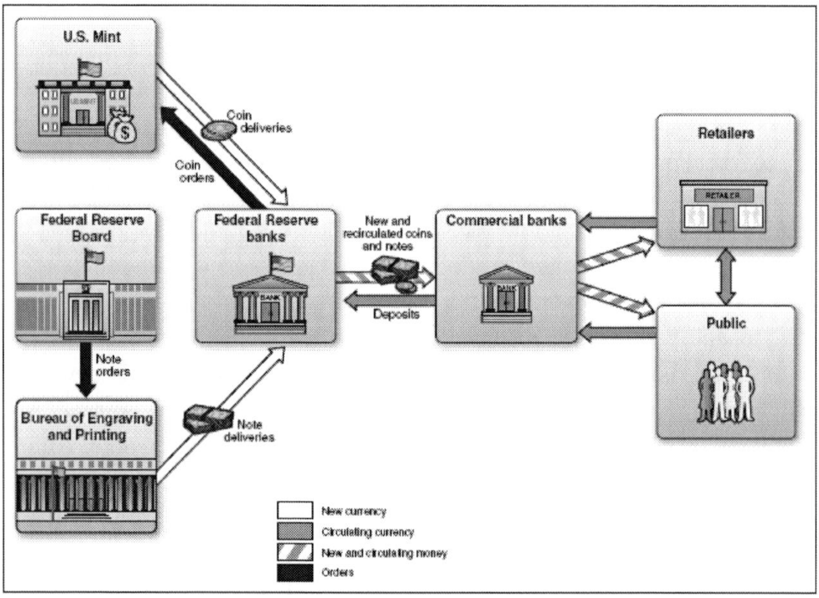

Source: GAO.

Figure 1. Production and Circulation of Notes and Coins.

Table 1. Number of $1 Coins Produced, 1979-2009

Coin design	Number produced as of November 2009	Production years
Susan B. Anthony	932 million	1979-1982 and 1999-2000
Sacagawea	1,467 million	2000-2008
Presidential series	1,722 million	2007-ongoing
Native American series	92 million	2009-ongoing
Total	4,213 million	

Source: Mint.

Note: The Eisenhower $1 coin was minted from 1971-1978; production figures are not readily available.

Currently, there are five different $1 coin designs in circulation—the Eisenhower coin, the Susan B. Anthony coin, the Sacagawea coin, the Presidential $1 coin series, and the Native American $1 coin series.[6] Table 1 shows production figures for the four $1 coin designs produced since 1979.

The four recent $1 coin designs are the same size and weight and have the same electromagnetic properties. The Susan B. Anthony $1 coin is silver in color, while the Sacagawea, Presidential, and Native American $1 coins are golden in color. The golden color was introduced in 2000 so that the public could better distinguish the $1 coins from the quarter, which the Susan B. Anthony $1 coin resembles and with which it is often confused.

The number of $1 coins shipped from the Mint to Federal Reserve banks peaked at over 1 billion in 2000, when the Sacagawea coin was first minted, and immediately declined to about 100 million coins in 2001. The number of $1 coins shipped averaged less than 50 million annually from 2002 through 2006, until the Presidential coin series was initiated in 2007. (See Figure 2.) About 1.1 billion $1 coins are held in storage by the Federal Reserve banks because, according to senior Federal Reserve officials, of the limited public demand.

In recent years, Congress sought to increase the circulation of the $1 coin, but circulation has remained limited. To remove barriers to circulation, the Presidential $1 Coin Act of 2005, among other things (1) mandated the use of $1 coins by federal agencies, the United States Postal Service, all transit agencies receiving federal funds, and all entities operating businesses, including vending machines, on U.S. government premises; (2) required the Mint to promote $1 coins to the public; and (3) required the Secretary of the Treasury, in consultation with the Federal Reserve, to review the co-circulation of the different $1 coin designs and make recommendations to Congress on improving the circulation of $1 coins.[7] Even with efforts taken to implement the legislation, the Federal Reserve banks had an inventory of about 1.1 billion $1 coins as of December 2010, which is sufficient inventory to cover the current level of public demand for the coin for over 13 years.

Other countries have introduced coins of similar value into circulation by replacing the corresponding notes, eventually leaving the public with no alternative to the coin of that value. Among the rationales for replacing notes with coins cited by foreign government officials and experts are the cost savings to governments derived from lower production costs and the decline over time of the purchasing power of currency due to inflation.[8] In 1985, for example, the Canadian House of Commons estimated that the conversion to a $1 coin would save the government $175 million (Canadian) in total over 20 years because it would no longer have to regularly replace worn out $1 notes. Canadian officials later determined that the Canadian government saved $450 million (Canadian) between 1987 and 1991.

Over the last 47 years, Australia, Canada, France, Japan, the Netherlands, New Zealand, Norway, Russia, Spain, and the UK, among others, have replaced lower-denomination notes with coins.

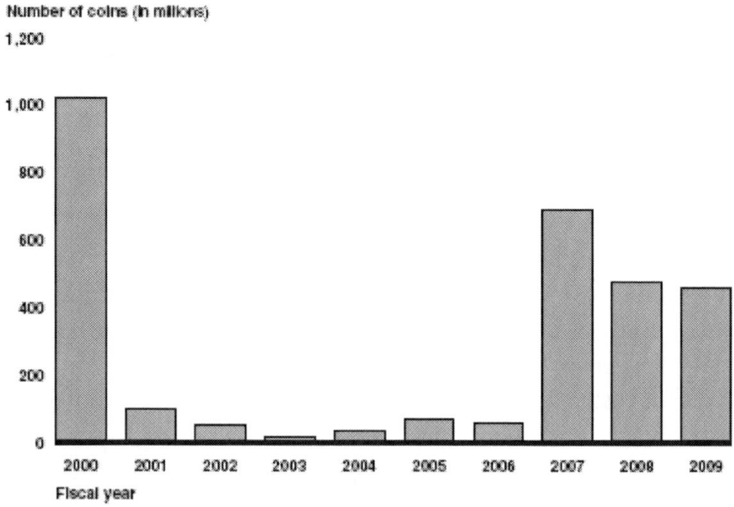

Source: GAO analysis of Mint data.

Figure 2. Number of $1 Coins Shipped from the Mint to Federal Reserve Banks, Fiscal Years 2000 through 2009.

Most of these replacements occurred in the 1980s. (Table 2 indicates when selected countries replaced notes with coins.)

In past work we reported that the annual net benefit to the government of replacing the $1 note with a $1 coin would be about $318 million (1990), $395 million (1993), $456 million (1995), and $522 million (2000).[9] Based on the experiences of other countries and the potential financial net benefit to the government, we have twice recommended that Congress provide for the elimination of the $1 note to ensure the success of $1 coin initiatives.[10]

Table 2. Selected Countries that Replaced Notes with Coins

Country	Note replaced	Year of replacement	U.S. value as of December 31, 2010
Australia	1 dollar	1984	$1.04
	2 dollar	1988	2.08
Canada	1 dollar	1987	1.02
	2 dollar	1996	2.04
France	5 franc	1970	NA[a]
	10 franc	1975	NA[a]
Japan	500 yen	1982	5.96
Netherlands	5 guilder	1988	NA[a]
New Zealand	1 dollar	1990	1.34
	2 dollar	1990	2.68
Norway	5 krone	1964	0.81
	10 krone	1984	1.61
Russia	10 ruble	2009	0.32
Spain	100 peseta	1982	NA[a]
	200 peseta	1986	NA[a]
	500 peseta	1988	NA[a]
UK	1 pound	1983	1.56

Sources: GAO/GGD-93-56; Bank of Canada, Japan Mint, Bank of Russia, and U.S. Department of the Treasury.

[a] Because some countries have replaced their national currency with the euro, the U.S. dollar value of currencies used prior to the euro can not be determined.

Replacing the $1 Notewith a $1 Coin Could Save the GovernmentApproximately $5.5Billion in InterestExpense over 30Years

Replacing $1 Notes with $1 Coins Would Increase the Net Benefit to the Government over 30 Years

We estimate that replacing the $1 note with a $1 coin would provide a net benefit to the government of approximately $5.5 billion over 30 years, amounting to an average yearly discounted net benefit[11] of about $184 million. However, this benefit would not be achieved evenly over the 30 years. In fact, as shown in figure 3, the federal government would incur a net loss during the first 4 years. Yearly net benefits begin to accrue in the fifth year of our analysis, and in the tenth year (2020), the initial start-up costs are paid back and overall net benefits begin to accrue. The early net loss represents the up-front cost of producing a large number of coins during the transition from notes to coins, together with the limited interest expense the government would avoid in the first few years after replacement began. While the estimated benefits in earlier GAO analyses were due to both seigniorage and reduced costs of coins (as compared to notes) over 30 years, our current net benefit estimate is solely due to seigniorage. In fact, the cost of producing coins for a full replacement is never fully recovered during the 30-year analysis, likely due to the longer note life and relatively higher cost of coin production today than was the case when our earlier studies were conducted. Moreover, our estimate, like all estimates, is uncertain, particularly in the later years, and thus the benefits could be greater or smaller than estimated. As a result, we have considered several alternative scenarios that are discussed later in this report and in appendix II.

To arrive at our estimate, we developed a model to examine the effects of replacing the $1 note with a $1 coin. We assumed that the replacement would be implemented starting in 2011, and during that year the Mint would invest in new equipment to increase its production capability for $1 coins. We also assumed that it would take 4 years for the Mint to produce enough coins to replace the currently outstanding dollar notes, and that during the transition, production of the paper note would stop.

Source: GAO analysis.

Note: The large net benefits in 2015 and 2016 occur because we assume that the Mint's production at maximum capacity during the 4-year transition period will lead to some overproduction and production drops dramatically in 2015 and 2016. Due to the far lower coin production costs, the net benefits to the government will temporarily spike in those years.

Figure 3. Discounted Net Benefit to the Government of Replacing $1 Notes with $1 Coins over 30 Years, by Year.

Our model assumptions cover a range of factors including the replacement ratio of coins to notes, the expected rate of growth in the demand for currency over 30 years, the costs of producing and processing both coins and notes, and the differential life span of coins and notes.[12] The cessation of production of $1 notes in our analysis might suggest a possible shortage of dollar currency during the transition. However, because of the existing $1 coins that the Federal Reserve banks hold and the rapid ramp up of production during the first 2 years of the transition, the outstanding dollar currency—both notes and coins—during the years of the transition equals or exceeds the demand we estimate for each of those years.

The assumption that contributed the most to the net benefit we estimated was the replacement ratio of coins to notes. Following the example of other countries that have replaced a note with a coin of equal value, we assumed that, because of differences in how people use these two forms of money, the public would need more than one coin for each note that had been in circulation. It is common for people to take coins out of their pockets and store them at the end of each day rather than retain them in their wallets as they do notes, for use the next day. These factors cause coins to circulate with less frequency than notes. Thus, for any given denomination of currency, a larger number of coins would need to be maintained in circulation to meet the public's demand for cash than would be needed if that denomination were provided in notes.

We previously reported that when Canada replaced its $1 note and the UK replaced its £1 note with a coin, both countries used a 1.6-to-1 replacement ratio. However, in both cases, once the transition was complete, coin production was very low or even nil in some years. Therefore, we determined that a 1.5-to-1 replacement rate would be appropriate for our analysis—low enough to avoid an excess of $1 coins without creating an undue risk of producing too few. Our analysis thus assumes that the number of $1 coins issued is 50 percent greater than the number of $1 notes that were in circulation. This assumption of increased production results in substantially increased seigniorage and accounts for our estimate of a net benefit to the government over the 30-year period of the analysis.

Our Current Estimate of the Yearly Net Benefit of Replacing the $1 Note with a $1 Coin is Lower than Previous Estimates for a Variety of Reasons

In 2000, we estimated that the yearly net benefit to the government of replacing the $1 note with a $1 coin would be roughly $522 million per year, after the replacement was complete. Our current estimate of an average yearly discounted net benefit to the government of about $184 million is lower than our previous estimate because of differences in the structure of our analysis and in our assumptions about the replacement ratio of coins to notes and the lifespan of the note.[13]

Structure of the Analysis

Our 2000 analysis estimated an annual level of net benefit to the government assuming that the transition to coins had already been completed. Hence, that analysis did not fully address the initial production costs of replacing all outstanding notes with coins. For the current analysis, we determined that the Mint would need to make various investments to produce substantially more new coins in relatively few years. We therefore assumed that the minting and distribution of new coins would substantially increase during a 4-year transition period and the production of $1 notes would cease. We included these increased coin production costs in the 30-year analysis.[14]

Lower Replacement Ratio

For our 2000 model, we assumed that, to meet society's needs, two $1 coins would be needed to replace each $1 note that had been in circulation. We arrived at that 2-to-1 replacement ratio based on the experience of other countries that had replaced their lowest-denomination note with a coin of the same denomination. Some of these countries used replacement ratios as high as 4 to 1. As we noted above, however, based on the experience of Canada and the UK, in our current model we used a replacement ratio of 1.5 to 1 because a higher ratio did not appear to be needed. Because a lower replacement ratio entails a reduced level of seigniorage, the net benefit to the government of switching to a $1 coin is lower in our current analysis than in our 2000 analysis. To examine the extent to which this assumption lowered our estimate, we ran our current model using the same 2-to-1 replacement ratio that we used in 2000 but maintained all other elements of our current model unchanged. This higher replacement ratio had the most impact on the estimated net benefit of the various sensitivity analyses we conducted. The average yearly discounted net benefit to the government would have been about $297 million, and the total net benefit over 30 years would have been about $8.9 billion if this higher replacement ratio had been used.

The Expanded Lifespan of the Note

Ten years ago, a $1 note lasted about 1.5 years on average. Because of improvements in the processing of paper notes, the life of the $1 note has grown considerably—to as high as 40 months on average, according to a BEP analysis.[15] This longer note life reduces the differential between the lives of the note and the coin, which is expected to have an average life of at least 30 years, according to senior Federal Reserve officials. To ascertain the extent to which the current longer life of a paper note led to a lower estimated net benefit to the government in our current analysis, we ran our model using the same 1.5- year average note life we used in the 2000 model, but retained all other elements of our current model. We found that if we had used the shorter note life in our current analysis, we would have estimated that the discounted net benefit to the government of a replacement would have been about $7.7 billion over the entire 30 years and the average yearly discounted net benefit would have been just over $256 million.

Our Current Estimate Would Vary with Changes in other Assumptions

Besides analyzing how differences in assumptions from our 2000 report affected our current estimate (our base case analysis) we analyzed alternative scenarios using the same model as we did for our base case analysis but altered certain assumptions. We compared our base case analysis to two alternative scenarios that relate to possible changes in how society uses money. In the first case, we assumed that the growing use of electronic payment mechanisms would erode society's use of cash over the period of our analysis. In the second case, we assumed that, rather than transferring all demand for the $1 note to the $1 coin, the public would prefer, and therefore demand, increased circulation of the $2 note as production of the $1 note ceased.

Reduced Growth in Demandfor Cash

In our base case, we assumed that the demand for cash would continue to grow with the growth in economic activity, as it has over many years. Even in the last several years, as the use of electronic means of payment has grown substantially, according to the Federal Reserve,[16] the demand for cash has continued to grow with the gross domestic product. However, further changes in the way Americans pay for goods at retail could lead to greater reliance on electronic payment methods. For example, some U.S. companies are planning to develop ways to make payments with a cell phone, a method that is already in use in some countries. If Americans come to rely more heavily on electronic payments, the demand for cash could grow more slowly in the future than we assume in our base case. For example, one possibility is that if the government replaces the $1 note with a $1 coin, electronic payments may increase as the public chooses to avoid the $1 coin. In this scenario, we assumed that the public would respond to the replacement of $1 notes with $1 coins by increasing its use of electronic payments, thereby reducing its demand for $1 currency by 20 percent.[17] In this scenario, we found that the net benefit to the government would be nearly $4.5 billion over 30 years and the average annual discounted net benefit would be nearly $149 million.

Replacement-Induced Demand for the $2 Note

If the $1 coin replaced the $1 note, the use of the $2 note could increase because people and businesses might limit how many coins they kept in their pockets and cash trays, and using the $2 note would help them do this. In Canada, demand for the $2 bill did increase when the $1 note was replaced with the $1 coin. However, Canada already had a readily circulating $2 note at the time, whereas the United States does not; therefore, we did not assume an increase in demand for the $2 note in our base case. In an alternative scenario, we assumed that 25 percent of the demand for cash that had been met with $1 notes would transfer to $2 notes and the remainder to $1 coins. Thus, the government would increase its production of $2 notes accordingly.[18]This scenario reduced the net benefit of the replacement because fewer new coins were produced and less seigniorage was generated. We found that the discounted net benefit to the government of replacement in this scenario would be slightly lower than our base case— about $5 billion over 30 years, for an average annual discounted net benefit of about $168 million.

The Model's Method of Estimating Net Benefit Differs from the Congressional Budget Office's Methodof Estimating How a Replacement Would Affectthe Federal Budget

Our estimate of the discounted net benefit to the government of replacing the $1 note with a $1 coin differs from the method that the Congressional

Budget Office (CBO) would use to calculate the impact on the budget of the same replacement. In the mid-1990s, CBO made such an estimate and noted that its findings for government savings were lower than our estimates at that time because of key differences in the two analyses. Most important, budget scorekeeping conventions do not factor in gains in seigniorage in calculating budget deficits.[19] Thus, the interest expense avoided in future years by reducing borrowing needs, which accounts for our estimate of net benefit to the government, would not be part of a CBO budget scoring analysis. Additionally, CBO's time horizon for analyzing the budget impact is up to 10 years—a much shorter time horizon than we use in our current analysis.

Replacement Could Increase CoinCounterfeiting Risk and Raise the Government's Deterrence Costs if Countermeasures Are Considered Necessary

Replacing the $1 note with a $1 coin could increase the risk of counterfeiting of the coin, which could increase the government's costs to deter counterfeiting if the risk were deemed large enough to warrant countermeasures. We did not include such costs in our estimate because counterfeiting of U.S. coins is currently minimal, both domestically and internationally, according to the U.S. Secret Service.[20] Moreover, counterfeit $1 notes accounted for less than 1 percent of all counterfeit U.S. notes detected in fiscal year 2009 (about 24,000 out of about 3 million). Nevertheless, senior officials at the Federal Reserve and Mint told us the increased circulation of $1 coins could increase the risk of counterfeiting, and senior Secret Service officials told us that counterfeiting of coins is an ongoing problem in the UK. A report by the UK's Royal Mint indicated a counterfeit rate of about 3 percent for £1 coins.[21]

In Canada, however, counterfeiting is minimal. Canadian officials told us that the total face value of the counterfeit Canadian $1 and $2 coins detected since the coins were introduced in 1987 and 1996, respectively, is about $10,000 (Canadian). Whether replacing the $1 note with a $1 coin in the United States would increase the risk of counterfeiting, as it apparently did in the UK, or whether it would remain low, as it has done in Canada, is unknown.

Both Canada and the UK created validation programs to maintain the integrity and quality of circulating coins after introducing the $1 coin and £1 coins, respectively. In both countries, when coins are returned from circulation as bank deposits, they are tested for authenticity, and heavily worn, bent, or otherwise unfit coins are identified and removed from circulation. Canada created its validation program when it introduced its $1 coin, while the UK created its program in response to a sharp increase in the counterfeiting of £1 coins. According to Canadian officials, the validation program was introduced to enable better management of Canada's coin inventories. The program provides information on the number of coins in circulation and allows for removing unfit coins from circulation, as well as for detecting counterfeit coins. The Federal Reserve banks circulate coins they receive from commercial banks, but do not have a comparable validation program. Coin processing companies run the coins through counting machines that, according to a processing company we interviewed, verify the denomination and genuineness of each coin. This process removes coins that the machines detect as unfit but does not represent a systematic application of criteria and standards of operation such as could be applied through a validation program managed by the Federal Reserve.

Public Acceptance of the $1 Coin Requires Production of the $1 Note to Cease

Our estimate of the net benefit to the government of replacing the $1 note with a $1 coin assumes that the $1 coin would be widely accepted and used by the public. In past work, we reported that the coin was not widely accepted and used. In 2002, we conducted a nationwide public opinion survey and found that the public was not using the $1 coin because people were familiar with the $1 note, the $1 coin was not widely available, and people did not want to carry around more coins.[22] In addition, 64 percent of the respondents to that survey were opposed to eliminating the $1 note. However, when respondents were told that such a replacement would save the government about half a billion dollars a year (our 2000 estimate), the proportion who said they opposed elimination of the note dropped to 37 percent. Two more recent national survey results suggest that opposition to eliminating the $1 note persists. For example, according to a Gallup poll conducted in 2006, 79 percent of respondents were opposed to replacing $1 notes with $1 coins, and their opposition decreased only slightly, to 64 percent, when they were asked to assume that a replacement would result in half a billion dollars in government savings each year.[23]

Efforts by the Mint to increase public acceptance and use of the $1 coin as it co-circulates with the $1 note have shown moderate success. To increase public acceptance and circulation of the $1 coin, the Presidential $1 Coin Act of 2005 requires the Mint to promote $1 coins to the public.[24] In response to the legislation, in 2008, the Mint conducted a pilot program in Austin, Texas; Portland, Oregon; Grand Rapids, Michigan; and Charlotte, North Carolina, to increase public acceptance of the $1 coin. Enlisting the support of national and local retailers, the Mint carried out advertising and public relations campaigns in which it promoted the $1 coin as recyclable, lasting for decades, and saving the nation money. As figure 4 shows, data collected as part of the pilot program show modest increases in the public's use of $1 coins in three of the four target markets as measured in public opinion surveys. Pilot program data also show that nationwide usage of the $1 coin declined during the period that the pilot study was conducted.

In past reports, we have noted that Congress and the executive branch would have to lead rather than follow public opinion for a transition from the $1 note to the $1 coin to succeed.[25]

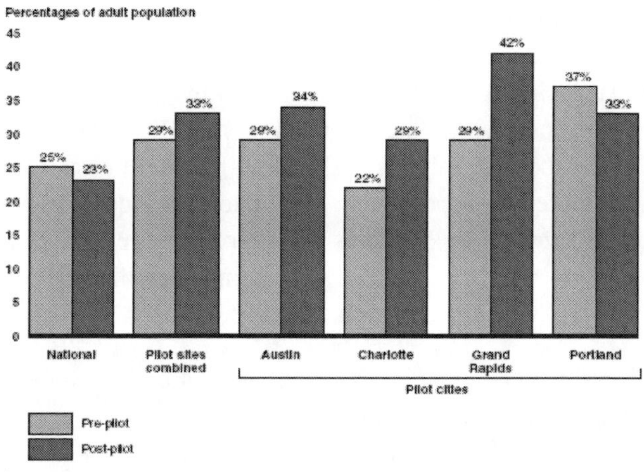

Source: Mint.

Figure 4. Use of $1 Coins in National and Target Markets before and after $1 Coin Pilot Program.

Furthermore, we have noted in those reports that past $1 coin initiatives—such as changes to the color of the $1 coin and new coin designs—have not led to widespread public acceptance and use, in part because the $1 note was not simultaneously eliminated. This point was reiterated by Canadian and UK officials we spoke with, who said that the only way to transition from note to coin is to stop producing the note. While observing that the public was resistant at first, they said that, with no alternative to the note, public dissatisfaction dissipated within a few years.

STAKEHOLDERS IDENTIFIED NEAR- AND LONG-TERM CHALLENGES TO THE PRIVATE SECTOR SHOULD THE $1 COIN REPLACE THE NOTE

Stakeholders representing a variety of retail and manufacturing industries and organizations that would be affected by a replacement identified two kinds of associated challenges and costs: (1) those that would result in the near term from the transition and (2) those that would result in the longer term from structural changes to the cost of doing business.[26] Most stakeholders we interviewed said, however, that they could not easily quantify the magnitude of these costs, and the majority noted that they would need 1 to 2 years to make the transition from $1 notes to $1 coins. Most stakeholders identified some likely benefits from replacing the $1 note with a $1 coin, including a financial benefit to the government. According to 13 of the 15 stakeholders we spoke with, replacing the $1 note with a $1 coin would involve various up-front, short-term costs during the transition period. Depending on the nature of their businesses, these stakeholders identified transition costs relating to their equipment, armored transportation, vault storage, and staff training. For example, all nine of the stakeholders we interviewed involved in retail sales, banking, and currency transport and processing identified equipment-related actions they would need to take, such as

- modifying vending and self-checkout machines, cash register drawers, and night depository equipment;
- upgrading armored trucks to carry the additional weight;
- acquiring hand trucks for moving coins within a business; and
- obtaining processing equipment such as coin counting and wrapping machines.

In addition, to accommodate higher volumes of $1 coins, five of the nine retail, banking, and armored carriers we interviewed said they would likely need to increase vault storage capacity. Some of the transitional costs and challenges may be more formidable than others. For example, increasing storage and transport capacity could entail additional investment, while modifying cash register drawers may involve primarily retooling the drawers.

Ten of the 15 stakeholders we spoke with also identified three areas in which the replacement of $1 notes with $1 coins might entail longer-term or ongoing costs: transportation, processing, and labor. For example, since coins are heavier than notes, 7 of 15 stakeholders said that their costs would likely increase because of higher transportation costs incurred by armored carriers from making additional trips or using more fuel with the heavier cargo. Moreover, two stakeholders noted that making additional trips to transport coins could increase security risks for staff. In addition, replacing the $1 note with a $1 coin might increase the number and types of personnel needed to physically handle coins and process them. Some stakeholders anticipated that any additional costs associated with $1 coins would be passed on to customers.

In contrast to the stakeholders who, as noted above, said that a replacement would mean higher short- and long-term costs for their businesses, two stakeholders we interviewed said that it might have only a minimal impact, particularly if the metal content of the $1 coin remained the same. According to officials from the National Automatic Merchandising Association, an organization representing the food and refreshment vending industry, many of its members have already modified their vending machines to accept all forms of payment, including coins, notes, and electronic transactions. Further, according to an association official, increased use of the $1 coin could be beneficial for the vending industry because it may reduce rejected sales due to old or damaged notes. He further noted that while the acceptance rate of notes has improved dramatically in vending, wider use of a $1 coin could improve consumer satisfaction. In addition, since transit agencies that receive federal funds were required under the Presidential $1 Coin Act of 2005 to accept and distribute $1 coins, many of the larger transit agencies have already modified their equipment to accept these coins, according to industry officials. For example, industry officials stated that New York City's Metropolitan Transportation Authority, which operates buses, subways, commuter trains, bridges, and tunnels in New York City and the surrounding area, is the largest user of $1 coins, with over 1,200 ticket vending machines that accept or dispense them.

CONCLUSION

As in the past, our analysis indicates that replacing the $1 note with a $1 coin would provide a financial benefit to the government if production of the $1 note ceased. However, the public continues to favor the $1 note over the $1 coin. In Canada and the UK, the public also preferred low-denomination notes to coins, but the governments nevertheless switched from notes to coins to achieve financial benefits. While the public resisted these transitions, opposition dissipated over time with no alternative to the note.

We have previously recommended to the Congress replacement of the $1 note with a $1 coin and, in view of the ongoing significant estimated federal financial benefit, continue to support this prior recommendation.

AGENCY COMMENTS AND OUR EVALUATION

We provided a draft of this report to the Federal Reserve, Treasury, and the Department of Homeland Security for their review and comment. The Federal Reserve and Treasury provided written comments, which are reproduced in appendix III and appendix IV, respectively, and technical comments, which we incorporated into the report as appropriate. The Department of Homeland Security had no comments. Both the Federal Reserve and Treasury maintained that an assessment of the benefits and costs to the U.S. economy—that included the net benefits to the government as we reported as well as the benefits and costs to the private sector—is important in any evaluation of whether to replace the $1 note with a $1 coin. We agree that the benefits and costs to the private sector are important considerations. However, we found no quantitative estimates that could be evaluated or modeled. As a result, we addressed the potential effect on the private sector through interviews with industries and organizations that might be affected by changes to currency. We obtained their views on the benefits and costs that might result from the replacement.

In addition, the Federal Reserve commented that if seignorage is not considered, the replacement of the $1 note with a $1 coin would result in a net *cost* to the government over 30 years, rather than a net benefit, as we reported. We agree with this statement—and point out in the report that the entire benefit of replacing the $1 note with a $1 coin would result from the seignorage. However, we believe that seignorage cannot be set aside since it is a result of issuing currency. The Federal Reserve also noted that the discounted net cost or benefit resulting from such a replacement would be influenced by assumptions about the length and cost of the initial transition and suggested that the report include sensitivity analyses that varied these assumptions. We included analyses that varied a number of assumptions and showed how our estimate would change. We did not include analyses that varied the length and cost of the transition because, at our request, the Mint provided us several scenarios of varying transition time periods and associated costs, which we assessed and used in our model.

We are sending copies of this report to interested congressional committees, the Secretaries of the Treasury and the Department of Homeland Security, and the Chairman of the Federal Reserve.

David J. Wise
Director, Physical Infrastructure Issues

APPENDIX I. OBJECTIVES, SCOPE, AND METHODOLOGY

We addressed the following questions: (1) What is the estimated net benefit, if any, to the government of replacing the $1 note with a $1 coin? (2) What other effects did stakeholders suggest such a replacement could have?

To estimate the net benefit to the government of replacing the $1 note with a $1 coin, we constructed an economic model, which we based on our analyses of past reports of GAO and the Board of Governors of the Federal Reserve System (Federal Reserve) that used an economic model to develop such an estimate, together with information obtained from reviews of agency documents and interviews with experts in government and academia. More specifically, we interviewed officials from the Federal Reserve, two bureaus of the Department of the Treasury (Treasury)—the Bureau of Engraving and Printing (BEP) and the United States Mint (Mint)—and the Department of Homeland Security's U.S. Secret Service to develop the structure, inputs, and assumptions for the model. Based on our document reviews and these interviews, we determined that the data used as inputs to our model for the production of notes and coins were sufficiently reliable for our analysis. We also interviewed officials from Canada and the United Kingdom (UK), both of which have replaced notes with coins, to gain information useful in determining certain key assumptions in our model. These included officials from the Bank of Canada, the Canadian Department of Finance, the Royal Canadian Mint, and the Royal Canadian Mounted Police's National Anti-Counterfeiting Bureau, as well as officials from the Royal Bank of England, the Royal Mint, and the Serious Organized Crime Agency. In addition, we interviewed four experts at federal agencies or academic institutions to obtain their views on our economic model. More detailed information on the structure, assumptions, and inputs of the economic model are found in appendix II.

To determine the various effects replacement could have on stakeholders, we identified industries and organizations that might be affected by changes to notes and coins.[1]Through a literature review and interviews with agency officials, we identified private companies involved in the production of materials for $1 notes and $1 coins. Because these entities would be affected by any increase or decrease in production, we interviewed the entities that produce the paper and ink for the $1 note (Crane Paper and SICPA Securink Corporation) and process metal for coins (Olin Brass and PMX Industries). Furthermore, through a review of literature and congressional testimonies, as well as interviews with agency officials, experts, and Canadian government officials, we identified other industries and interest groups that are intensive users of currency and might be affected by the replacement of the $1 note with the $1 coin. These entities included banks and financial institutions; grocery stores; convenience stores; fast food establishments; vending machine companies, including those that make the note and coin acceptors used in vending machines; armored carriers that process and transport currency; transit agencies; retailers, including companies that make cash register drawers; coin laundry establishments; and consumer and public advocacy groups. To ensure broad representation among these groups, we interviewed officials from the following organizations:

- American Banking Association,
- American Beverage Association,
- American Public Transit Association,
- Coin Laundry Association,
- Food Marketing Institute,
- MEI Group,
- National Association of Convenience Stores,
- National Armored Car Association,
- National Automatic Merchandising Association,
- National Cash Register Company,
- National Consumers League,
- National Federation of the Blind,
- National Franchisee Association,
- Wal-Mart, and
- $1 Coin Coalition.

Finally, to better understand the production, processing, and circulation of currency, we visited the BEP production facility in Washington, D.C.; the Mint production facility in Philadelphia, Pennsylvania; and an armored carrier note and coin processing facility in Baltimore, Maryland.

We conducted this performance audit from June 2010 to March 2011 in accordance with generally accepted government auditing standards. These standards require that we plan and perform the audit to obtain sufficient, appropriate evidence to provide a reasonable basis for our findings and conclusions based on our audit objectives. We believe that the evidence obtained provides a reasonable basis for our findings and conclusions based on our audit objectives.

APPENDIX II. DESIGN OF GAO'S ECONOMIC MODEL AND DETAILED RESULTS FOR THE BASE CASE AND ALTERNATIVE ASSUMPTIONS

This appendix summarizes information about the model we developed to estimate the net benefit to the government of replacing the $1 note with a $1 coin. Specifically, this appendix (1) describes the design of the model, including the assumptions used in it and their sources, and (2) presents detailed results of the model's analysis for our base case, in which we compare a replacement scenario with the status quo, and for two alternative scenarios.

Design of the Model

To estimate the net benefit to the government of replacing the $1 note with a $1 coin, we created a model that analyzes the benefits and costs to the government of issuing currency—including both notes and coins—under different scenarios and assumptions over 30 years.[1] The government derives a benefit from issuing coins, known as seigniorage—a term wealso apply to notes to mean, for both, the difference between the face value of currency and its production costs. Seigniorage reduces the government's need to borrow, allowing it to avoid interest on debt that it would otherwise incur.

Base Case

To estimate the net benefit to the government of replacing the $1 note witha $1 coin, we designed our model to calculate the difference between the baseline and a replacement scenario. Specifically, because the government receives a net benefit from issuing both notes and coins, we calculated the net benefits under the status quo, in which most demand for $1 currency is provided by notes (as is currently the case), and a replacement scenario, in which notes cease to be produced and are replaced by $1 coins. The difference between the net benefits under these two scenarios is the net benefit to the government.

For the status quo, we assume that notes remain the dominant form of currency at the $1 denomination. The Mint continues to produce $1 coins at current levels, but not all of them enter circulation.

- Currently, about 1 billion of the approximately 4 billion $1 coins that the Mint has produced since it started minting the Susan B. Anthony $1 coin in 1979 are stored with the Federal Reserve. We do not count these coins as contributing toward the net benefit to the government because these coins are not being held by the public, and therefore, governmentwide, there has not been a financial gain.[2]
- We assume that the remaining 3 billion $1 coins are held by the public. We also assume that some of these remaining $1 coins are lost or not in active circulation.
- Based on current projections, which incorporate the legislative requirements for producing Presidential and Native American $1 coins, we assume that the Mint will continue to manufacture more coins than the public demands until it completes its production of Presidential $1 coins, currently scheduled through part of 2016. In our baseline scenario we assume that production of the $1 coin essentially ceases after 2016.[3] BEP officials commented that it is unrealistic to assume the Mint will cease $1 coin production after 2016. However, we have no basis on which to make an assumption about the level of $1 coin production after the completion of the Presidential series. As such, we assume that coins stop being produced after the series is complete. The small level of demand for $1 coins will be able to be satisfied by coins on hand at Federal Reserve banks for many years after that time.[4]

For our replacement scenario, we assume a 4-year transition period during which

- the production of $1 notes stops immediately;
- no $1 notes are withdrawn from circulation, but due to their short life, they would naturally fall out of circulation within a few years;
- the 1 billion coins currently stored with the Federal Reserve are released into circulation in the first year;
- 1 billion $1 coins that were inactive and held by the public enter active circulation in the first year; and
- the Mint expands its production of $1 coins during the first 4 years. During the transition period, we assume the Mint's coin production and the government's associated costs both increase.
- In the first year, the Mint not only increases its production to its current maximum capacity, but also modifies other coin production lines to produce more $1 coins.
- By the second year, the Mint is able to produce at a new maximum capacity and does so throughout the 4-year transition period until it has produced enough $1 coins to replace all $1 notes in circulation.
- These efforts by the Mint to expand its production of $1 coins increase its costs during the transition period.

In addition, we assume that the government incurs costs to publicize the shift from $1 notes to $1 coins and that the variable costs of producing higher-denomination notes increase after the BEP loses some degree of economies of scale that it currently derives from producing $1 notes. For example, if BEP is unable to purchase certain supplies such as ink and paper in quantities as large as it does now, it may cause the vendors to raise their prices.

After the 4-year transition period, we assume that the Mint reduces its production of $1 coins to an amount sufficient to offset attrition and meet the growth in demand for currency. As a result, the Mint's coin production costs decline.

To calculate our estimate, we relied on data from several sources, including the Mint, BEP, and the Federal Reserve. We also interviewed relevant officials from international governments and outside experts. All assumptions used in the model are projections of future conditions, hypothetical actions, or both.

Table 3. Assumptions, Values, Sources, and Rationales Used in the Model

Assumption	Value	Source(s)/rationale
Government borrowing rate	About 5.4 percent (varies by year)	We used the average of the 3-month Treasury bill and 10-year Treasury note rates as forecast by the Congressional Budget Office (CBO).
Discount rate	About 3.4 percent (varies by year)	We used the government borrowing rate (above) minus the level of inflation projected by CBO. This provides a real discount rate, which we use because all of the numbers in the analysis are in real terms.
Growth rate of $1 currency	About 3.3 percent (varies by year)	We assumed that the demand for notes would grow at a rate between the real and nominal gross domestic product growth rates. This appears to have been the pattern over the last decade, based on Federal Reserve data. In the replacement scenario, we assume the demand for coins grows at the same rate as demand for notes would have grown. In the baseline scenario, we assume negligible demand for the coin after the end of the Presidential coin series.
Replacement ratio	1.5 coins to 1 note	As in our previous studies, we assumed that coins would circulate more slowly than notes and, therefore, more than one coin would be needed to satisfy the demand for one note. Based on our study of experience in Canada and the UK, we used a 1.5- to-1 replacement ratio for our base case. Canada produced 1.6 coins for each note during the transition; once the transition was complete, production was very low or even nil in some years. Because underproduction is a greater risk to the economy than overproduction, we adjusted the ratio downward by only a small amount.
Lifespan of notes	Median of 40 months (19 percent annual attrition rate)	Our analysis of data from BEP and the Federal Reserve indicates an average lifespan for notes of 32 to 40 months. We chose the upper end of that range because of upcoming process changes at the Federal Reserve that are expected to increase the lifespan of notes.
Lifespan of coins	Median of approximately 34 years (2 percent annual attrition rate)	Testimony from the Mint and international experts put the average life of coins at about 30 years. A study of coin attrition rates found a 2.5 percent annual rate for quarters and showed attrition decreasing as coin value increased.
Variable cost of notes	2.7 cents per note	Based on our analysis of 11 years of cost and production data, as well asinformation on the long-run variability of certain cost categories provided by BEP.
Variable cost of coins	15 cents per coin	Based on our analysis of 10 years of cost and production data provided by the Mint. Specifically, we regressed the total production costs on a constant and the number of notes produced. We use the coefficient on the number produced as the estimate of variable cost.

Table 3. (Continued)

Time frame	2011 through 2040	We estimated the net benefit to the government over 30 years, as requested. Weassumed the policy would go into effect at the beginning of 2011 and discounted all values to this base year. We assumed that the period from 2011 through 2014 would be a transition period.
Note processing cost	Approximately 0.3 cents per note	We used 4 years of data (2006–2009) from the Federal Reserve, which included total direct processing costs and the number of notes processed
Coin processing cost	Approximately 0.01cents per coin	We used 4 years of data (2006–2009) from the Federal Reserve, which included total direct processing costs and the number of coins processed. We did not include additional costs to authenticate coins under the replacement scenario, since it is unknown if such a process would be put in place and we have no basis for determining a reasonable cost
Note processing frequency	1.3 times per year per note	We used data provided by the Federal Reserve.
Coin processing frequency	0.1 times per year per coin	We used data provided by the Federal Reserve. It is possible that processing frequency would change in a replacement scenario, but we have no basis for a projection.
Initial number of $1 notes in circulation	Approximately 9.5 billion	Based on Federal Reserve data and our growth projection described above.
Initial number of $1 coins in circulation	3 billion held by the public; 1 billion stored with the Federal Reserve	Based on data from the Mint and the Federal Reserve. We assumed that there are 3 billion coins held by the public. Some have been lost and some are not actively in circulation. We assume that 1 billion of these coins enter active circulation in the replacement scenario.
Increase in BEP variable costs	— [a]	Based on data provided by BEP and its suppliers.
Cost to Mint to convert production lines	Approximately $8 million	Based on data from the Mint.
Public awareness campaign	Approximately $7.8 million	We assumed a public awareness campaign would be conducted to inform the public during the first year of the transition period. We used an estimate provided by the Mint for a previous GAO report, updated for inflation.[b]
Production of and demand for $1 coins in the base case	380 million produced per year through 2016; approximately 200 million enter public holdings per year	Based on projections provided by the Mint. We assumed that those coins that are not held by the public are returned to the Federal Reserve.

Source: GAO analysis of agencies' data.

[a]Data are proprietary.

[b]GAO/GGD-90-88.

Therefore, some uncertainty is inevitable, particularly for elements of the assumptions that occur farther in the future. Moreover, some assumptions reflect our analysis of data. We discussed our assumptions with relevant stakeholders and experts to verify that our analysis is reasonable. Table 3 lists the values, sources, and rationales for some key assumptions.

Detailed Results Using the Base Caseand Alternative Assumptions

ResultsUsing Base Case Assumptions

Compared to continuing the status quo, replacing the $1 note with a $1 coin would increase the government's net benefit by approximately $5.5 billion over 30 years, or about $184 million annually, on average, in net present value terms. This average masks significant variation over the 30- year period of our analysis. In the first few years, a replacement would cause a net loss because the cost of producing so many coins would be large. This early net loss represents the up-front cost of producing a large number of coins during the transition from notes to coins together with the limited interest expense the government would avoid in the first few years after replacement began.

While the estimated benefits in earlier GAO analyses were due to both seigniorage and reduced costs of coins (as compared to notes) over 30 years, our current net benefit estimate is solely due to seigniorage. In fact, the cost of producing coins for a full replacement is never fully recovered during the 30-year analysis, likely due to the longer note life and relatively higher cost of coin production today than was the case when our earlier studies were conducted. Moreover, our estimate, like all estimates, is uncertain, particularly in the later years, and thus the benefits could be greater or smaller than estimated. (See fig. 3 in the body of our report and table 4 at the end of this appendix.)

ResultsUsing Alternative Assumptions

Under alternative assumptions, our estimate of the net benefit to the government of a replacement would change. Table 4 shows how changes in two assumptions—the demand for currency and the replacement ratio of coins to notes—would affect our estimate. We conducted several additional alternative analyses, and are presenting these two, which provide the greatest range of benefits. In each of the alternative scenarios, we changed one assumption and held all other values constant.

Table 4. Comparison of Benefit Estimates under Base Case and Alternative AssumptionsDollars in Billions

Key assumption	Base case	Replacement-induced demand decline	Higher replacement ratio
Lifespan of note, in months	40	40	40
Replacement ratio of coins to notes	1.5 to 1	1.5 to 1	2.0 to 1
Annual growth in demand for currency	About 3.3 %	About 3.3% baseline and 2.6 % replacement	About 3.3%
Status quo			
Billions of notes produced over 30 years	109	109	109
Billions of coins produced over 30 years	2	2	2
Present value of reduction in government interest payments, over 30 years	$10.8	$10.8	$10.8
Present value of note production and processing costs, over 30 years	$2.1	$2.1	$2.1
Present value of coin production and processing costs, over 30 years	$0.3	$0.3	$0.3
Total net benefit to the government of status quo	$8.4	$8.4	$8.4
Replacement			
Billions of notes produced over 30 years	0	0	0
Billions of coins produced over 30 years	50	41	67
Present value of reduction in government interest payments, over 30 years	$19.7	$17.9	$24.7
Present value of note production and processing costs, over 30 years [a]	$0.2	$0.2	$0.2
Present value of coin production and processing costs, over 30 years [b]	$5.6	$4.8	$7.2
Total net benefit to the government of replacement	$13.9	$12.9	$17.3
Net benefit to government of replacement over 30 years	$5.5	$4.5	$8.9

Source: GAO analysis.

Note: Totals may not add because of rounding.

[a]Under the replacement, no notes are produced, but limited ongoing processing costs are borne in the first few years.

[b]The replacement incorporates certain costs associated with issuing coins that are not included in the base case, such as the costs of modifying equipment at the Mint to expand its production of $1 coins during the transition period, losing economies of scale at BEP after it stops producing $1 notes, and conducting a public information campaign to publicize the new $1 coins.

In the first alternative scenario, the replacement of notes with coins causes a decrease in the demand for currency as people switch to electronic means of payment. Specifically, the demand for currency grows at a rate equal to 80 percent of the growth of demand for notes in the baseline scenario. Using this assumption, our estimate of the net benefit tothe government decreases to $4.5 billion over 30 years, which is a decrease of about $1 billion from our base case.

In the second alternative scenario, we changed the number of coins needed to replace each note in circulation. Changing our estimate of the replacement ratio of coins to notes from our current estimate of 1.5 to 1 to our 2000 estimate of 2.0 to 1 increases the net benefit to the government to about $8.9 billion over 30 years, or about $3.4 billion more than our base case estimate.

Table 4 provides detailed results of our model's analysis using our basecase and these two alternative assumptions.

Appendix III. Comments from the Board of Governors of the Federal Reserve System

BOARD OF GOVERNORS
OF THE
FEDERAL RESERVE SYSTEM
WASHINGTON, D.C. 20551

LOUISE L. ROSEMAN
DIRECTOR
DIVISION OF
RESERVE BANK OPERATIONS
AND PAYMENT SYSTEMS

February 14, 2011

Mr. David Wise
Director
Physical Infrastructure Issues
U.S. Government Accountability Office
441 G Street, N.W.
Washington, D.C. 20548

Dear Mr. Wise:

Thank you for the opportunity to comment on the GAO's draft report "*U.S. Coins: Replacing the $1 Note with a $1 Coin Would Provide a Financial Benefit to the Government.*" In the report, the GAO concludes that there would be a net benefit to the federal government from the replacement of $1 notes to $1 coins, due to the increased seigniorage revenue. Setting seigniorage aside and considering only the real costs to the government, the report concludes that replacing the $1 note with a $1 coin results in a net *cost* to the government over a 30-year period.

Although the GAO was asked to evaluate benefits to the government, we believe an assessment of the benefits and costs to the U.S. economy more broadly is an important consideration in evaluating whether to replace the $1 note with a $1 coin. Seigniorage would not be a factor in such an analysis, since it is a revenue transfer from the private sector to the government. The report notes (but does not quantify) the near- and long-term challenges to the private sector should the $1 coin replace the $1 note. A societal cost-benefit analysis would include the costs and benefits not only to the government but also to the banking industry, retailers, the Federal Reserve, consumers, and others to handle $1 coins and $1 notes. Also, the discounted net cost or benefit of a replacement of $1 notes by $1 coins is influenced significantly by the assumptions regarding the initial transition period and cost. A sensitivity analysis in the final report that varies those transition assumptions would provide useful context.

We have provided technical comments on the draft report under separate cover.

Sincerely,

Email: Louisa.Roseman@frb.gov
Phone (202) 452-2789 • Fax: (202) 452-2746

APPENDIX IV. COMMENTS FROM THE DEPARTMENT OF THE TREASURY

DEPARTMENT OF THE TREASURY
WASHINGTON, D.C. 20220

February 18, 2011

Mr. David Wise
Director, Physical Infrastructure Issues
Government Accountability Office
441 G St., NW
Washington, DC 20548

Dear Mr. Wise:

Thank you for the opportunity to review and comment on the General Accountability Office's (GAO) draft report "Replacing the $1 Note with a $1 Coin Would Provide a Financial Benefit to the Government" (GAO-11-281).

The Treasury Department has reviewed the report in consultation with the Bureau of Engraving and Printing and the U.S. Mint and would like to provide feedback for clarification. In this review, several technical issues were cited concerning certain assumptions, definitions, and statements. The attached document highlights these concerns and is provided for your consideration in preparing the final report.

As noted in the draft report, GAO's study did not consider some factors that were outside the scope of the financial benefit to the Government, such as environmental impacts. Furthermore, we note that GAO acknowledged that societal costs would accompany any such transition, but these costs were not included because GAO could not quantify them adequately. The government, of course, must consider these more holistic factors in any broader discussion of the report's recommendations.

Additionally, please note that the Federal Reserve will be revising its processing methodology for $1 notes shortly after the publication of this report. The new process is expected to significantly reduce the premature destruction of fit (acceptable) $1 notes when they are processed at the Federal Reserve Banks. As a consequence, the life of a $1 note in circulation is expected to increase significantly, reducing the estimated savings from replacing the $1 note with the $1 coin.

Sincerely,

Rosie Rios
Treasurer of the United States

Attachment 1: Technical Comments

End Notes

[1] GAO, National Coinage Proposals: Limited Public Demand for New Dollar Coin or Elimination of Pennies, GAO/GGD-90-88 (Washington, D.C.: May 23, 1990); 1-Dollar Coin: Reintroduction Could Save Millions If Properly Managed, GAO/GGD-93-56 (Washington, D.C.: Mar. 11, 1993); Dollar Coin Could Save Millions, GAO/T-GGD-95-203 (Washington, D.C.: July 13, 1995); and Financial Impact of Issuing the New $1 Coin, GAO/GGD-00-111R (Washington, D.C.: Apr. 7, 2000).

[2] GAO/GGD-00-111R.

[3] We are assuming a status quo tax structure.

[4] 12 U.S.C. §418.

[5] 31 U.S.C. §5111(a)(1).

[6] In 2007, the Mint, upon direction by Congress, began issuing four $1 coins per year featuring images of past Presidents in the order they served. In 2009, the Mint, upon direction by Congress, began issuing $1 coins featuring designs celebrating the important contributions made by Indian tribes and individual Native Americans to the history and development of the United States. For both the Presidential series and the Native American series, the design on the back of the coins rotates, while the obverse (heads side) continues to feature either a president or Sacagawea, respectively.

[7] 31 U.S.C. §5112(p).

[8] For example, the U.S. dollar now has the purchasing power that a quarter had in 1975.

[9] GAO/GGD-90-88, GAO/GGD-93-56, GAO/T-GGD-95-203, and GAO/GGD-00-111R.

[10] GAO/GGD-90-88 and GAO/GGD-93-56.

[11] A discounted net value uses a rate, known as the discount rate, to convert the value of payments or receipts expected in future years to today's value, taking into account that the further into the future an amount is paid or received, the smaller its value is today. Applying a discount rate establishes a consistent basis for comparing alternative investments that will have differing patterns of costs and benefits over many years.

[12] We recognize that societal costs—such as the costs to banks, retailers, and other extensive users of cash—exist in addition to the cost to government, but we could not quantify them adequately to add to our analysis.

[13] Our 2000 estimate is in 2000 dollars, while our current estimate is in 2011 dollars. The gross domestic product price index rose by 25 percent between 2000 and 2010, which means that the value of the difference between the two estimates is higher than the nominal difference between these numbers, since the 2000 value, if inflated to 2011 dollars, would be 25 percent higher.

[14] Our 1990 analysis more closely resembled the current analysis in that it more fully included start-up costs in a 30-year analysis. That study estimated an average annual discounted net benefit to the government of $318 million (in 1990 dollars) over 30 years.

[15] Treasury and Federal Reserve officials said that additional improvements in the processing of $1 notes in spring 2011 are expected to further increase the lifespan of the $1 note.

[16] According to the Federal Reserve, the number of electronic payments increased from 2006 through 2009, with debit card usage growing at double-digit annual rates. While the study did not measure cash usage, it concluded that it is likely that some of the debit card growth has come from its substitution for cash payments. *The 2010 Federal Reserve Payments Study, Noncash Payment Trends in the United States: 2006-2009*, sponsored by the Federal Reserve System (Dec. 8, 2010).

[17] The Federal Reserve did not provide us with a projection of a change in the demand for cash based on electronic payments and we did not have any evidence to suggest how much demand might transfer to electronic use, but a 20 percent transfer to electronic use would appear to be a reasonably substantial change in the public's use of money.

[18] This is the same assumption made in our 1990 report.

[19] Budget scorekeeping is the process of estimating the budgetary effects of pending and enacted legislation and comparing them with limits set in the budget resolution or legislation. A budget resolution sets forth an overall budget plan for Congress against which individual appropriations bills, other appropriations, and revenue measures are to be evaluated. Scorekeeping tracks data such as budget authority, receipts, outlays, the surplus or deficit, and the public debt limit.

[20] Among other things, the U.S. Secret Service is responsible for safeguarding the nation's financial infrastructure and payment systems to preserve the integrity of U.S. currency. This includes reducing the amount of counterfeit currency in circulation domestically and abroad.

[21] The Royal Mint, *Royal Mint Trading Fund Group Annual Report 2009-10* (London, UK: July 26, 2010).

[22] GAO, *U.S. Coins: Public Views on Changing Coin Design*, GAO-03-206 (Washington, D.C.: Dec. 17, 2002).

[23] Gallup News Service, *Americans Support Dollar Coins Featuring Past Presidents* (Princeton, New Jersey: Nov. 21, 2006). For the survey results reported by Gallup, one can say with 95 percent confidence that the maximum margins of sampling error are +/- 5 percentage points. In addition to sampling error, question wording and practical difficulties in conducting surveys can introduce error or bias into the findings of public opinion polls. We could not evaluate the accuracy of these poll results based on the information available to us.

[24] Pub.L. No. 109-145, §104, 119 Stat. 2670 (2005).

[25] GAO/GGD-90-88, GAO/GGD-93-56, and GAO/GGD-00-111R.

[26] BEP officials pointed out that replacing the $1 note with a $1 coin would also have environmental impacts relating to obtaining raw materials and carbon dioxide emissions, among others. We did not assess the potential environmental effects of a switch.

End Note for Appendix I

[1] We did not assess the environmental impacts, such as those relating to obtaining raw materials and carbon dioxide emissions, which replacement could have.

End Notes for Appendix II

[1] We use the term "benefit" rather than revenue because we consider the income from an economic standpoint instead of a budget scoring standpoint. This is consistent with past GAO work on this issue. A replacement would also have benefits and costs for private businesses and for the general public and consumers, but our model is not designed to estimate these effects.

[2] The Mint recognizes the seigniorage as soon as the coins are transferred to the Federal Reserve for initial distribution, even if the coins do not necessarily enter active circulation. However,

because the Treasury will not have a reduced need to issue debt until coins are put into public circulation, we treat the actualization of seigniorage as occurring at that time. It is only when debt issuance is reduced that the benefit of saved interest expense begins to accrue.

[3] The Mint has indicated that it will continue to produce Native American $1 coins after it completes the Presidential series, but given the current stockpile of $1 coins stored with the Federal Reserve and the modest public demand, production is expected to be limited.

[4] To the extent that some coins need to be minted to meet demand much later, that would add costs to the baseline scenario and would increase the calculated net benefits of a replacement by a small amount.

INDEX

A

accountability, 23, 53
accounting, 28, 48
advocacy, 76
agencies, 3, 9, 57, 61, 73, 75, 76, 81
annual rate, 80, 86
appropriations, 87
assessment, 74
attitudes, 16
audit, 4, 39, 53, 58, 77
authenticity, 2, 12, 60, 69
authority, 87
awareness, 81

B

Bank of Canada, 14, 22, 63, 75
Bank of England, 75
banking, 25, 58, 72
banking sector, 25
banks, 17, 25, 26, 27, 33, 59, 61, 65, 70, 76, 78, 86
barriers, 27, 61
base, 33, 67, 68, 77, 80, 81, 83, 84
base year, 81
benefits, 2, 3, 4, 6, 7, 8, 11, 13, 16, 20, 36, 37, 39, 40, 42, 43, 47, 48, 53, 56, 63, 64, 72, 74, 77, 78, 82, 86, 87, 88
bias, 87
bird design, 16
budget deficit, 8, 69
budget resolution, 12, 87
Bureau of Engraving and Printing, 55, 58, 75
businesses, 4, 9, 10, 19, 20, 21, 26, 27, 58, 61, 68, 72, 73, 87

C

campaigns, 71
Canadian government, 3, 10, 16, 17, 62, 76
carbon, 53, 87
carbon dioxide, 53, 87
cash, 3, 7, 8, 11, 12, 14, 15, 22, 42, 47, 48, 57, 58, 59, 65, 67, 68, 72, 76, 86, 87
central bank, 59
challenges, 4, 32, 72
circulation, 3, 4, 6, 9, 10, 12, 13, 14, 15, 16, 17, 18, 19, 21, 24, 28, 34, 38, 39, 40, 47, 53, 57, 59, 61, 65, 66, 67, 69, 71, 77, 78, 79, 81, 84, 87
City(ies), 15, 73
color, 9, 61, 71
commerce, 15, 18, 20, 59
commercial, 12, 59, 70
commercial bank, 12, 59, 70
commodity, 32, 33
common sense, 18
communication, 33

community, 10
Congress, 2, 3, 11, 22, 23, 24, 32, 34, 53, 61, 62, 71, 74, 86, 87
Congressional Budget Office, 8, 42, 53, 55, 68, 69, 80
consumers, 16, 19, 20, 21, 26, 87
controversial, 3
copper, 14
corrosion, 34
cost, vii, 2, 3, 6, 7, 8, 9, 10, 11, 12, 13, 16, 17, 20, 21, 27, 31, 32, 34, 35, 36, 37, 38, 39, 42, 43, 47, 48, 49, 53, 59, 61, 64, 72, 74, 80, 81, 82, 86
cost saving, 3, 10, 16, 17, 31, 49, 61
costs of production, 6, 39
cotton, 28
counterfeiting, 14, 49, 69, 70
currency, viii, 2, 4, 6, 8, 10, 11, 12, 14, 15, 18, 25, 38, 39, 40, 43, 47, 49, 56, 58, 59, 61, 63, 65, 68, 72, 74, 76, 77, 78, 79, 80, 82, 83, 87
customers, 13, 14, 16, 17, 18, 27, 73

D

database, 14
deficit, 87
Democrat, 23
Department of Homeland Security, 58, 74, 75
Department of the Treasury, 4, 48, 55, 58, 63, 75
deposits, 12, 27, 60, 69
direct processing costs, 81
dissatisfaction, 10, 72
distribution, 15, 16, 66, 87
DNA, 14
draft, 37, 48, 56, 74
ductility, 34
durability, 4

E

economic activity, 67
economic growth, 26, 59
economies of scale, 79, 83
electromagnetic, 34, 61
e-mail, 49
employees, 31
end-users, 15
engineering, 18
England, 75
environment, 42, 48
environmental effects, 87
environmental impact, 37, 48, 53, 87
equipment, 2, 3, 6, 7, 9, 10, 17, 24, 40, 57, 64, 72, 73, 83
erosion, 19
evidence, 4, 12, 24, 39, 59, 77, 87
executive branch, 71
expertise, 15, 18
exposure, 33

F

fast food, 76
federal funds, 9, 61, 73
federal government, vii, 1, 2, 4, 6, 12, 21, 38, 39, 53, 59, 63
Federal Reserve, 2, 4, 7, 19, 20, 22, 25, 26, 34, 37, 38, 40, 42, 48, 49, 50, 56, 58, 59, 61, 62, 65, 67, 69, 70, 74, 75, 78, 79, 80, 81, 84, 86, 87, 88
financial, vii, viii, 1, 2, 3, 4, 6, 11, 12, 15, 19, 23, 24, 35, 37, 39, 48, 55, 56, 58, 59, 62, 72, 73, 74, 76, 78, 87
financial institutions, 15, 19, 58, 76
financial reports, 24
fiscal year 2009, 32, 69
fitness, 60
food, 9, 73, 76
forecasting, 15
France, 10, 25, 62, 63
funding, 53
funds, 53, 61, 73

G

GAO, vii, viii, 1, 2, 3, 5, 6, 11, 12, 20, 21, 22, 23, 24, 25, 27, 28, 35, 36, 37, 40, 41, 44, 45, 46, 49, 53, 55, 56, 57, 58, 60, 62, 63, 64, 75, 77, 81, 82, 83, 86, 87
government spending, 24
governments, 10, 37, 58, 59, 61, 74, 79
gross domestic product, 68, 80, 86
growth, 6, 32, 40, 59, 65, 67, 79, 80, 81, 83, 86
growth rate, 32, 80

H

hardness, 34
history, 18, 24, 31, 33, 86
House, 1, 13, 19, 23, 31, 61
human, 28

I

icon, 16
images, 86
immunity, 28
improvements, 17, 36, 67, 86
income, 20, 32, 33, 87
independence, 23
industry(ies), viii, 2, 4, 8, 9, 10, 14, 17, 18, 42, 56, 58, 72, 73, 74
inflation, 10, 12, 61, 80, 81
infrastructure, 87
institutions, 31, 58, 75, 76
integrity, 18, 53, 69, 87
interest groups, 16, 76
investment(s), 15, 32, 53, 66, 72, 86
investors, 33
issues, 6, 12, 19, 34, 39, 48, 53, 59

J

Japan, 10, 25, 62, 63

L

lead, 12, 15, 40, 44, 45, 46, 64, 68, 71
legislation, 12, 24, 28, 61, 71, 87
life expectancy, 6, 36, 40
linen, 28
loans, 20
local government, 48, 49
logistics, 24, 26
lower-denomination notes, viii, 55, 58, 62

M

magnitude, 9, 72
majority, 9, 72
management, 15, 70
manufacturing, 16, 18, 31, 72
marketing strategy, 33
marketplace, 16, 18, 27
Maryland, 77
materials, 58, 76, 87
matter, 23
metals, 32, 34
methodology, 4, 28, 59
missions, 33, 87
monopoly, 21
monopoly power, 21

N

national character, 19
Native Americans, 86
negative consequences, 47
Netherlands, 10, 25, 62, 63
neutral, 16
New Zealand, 10, 17, 25, 62, 63
nickel, 14, 32
Norway, 10, 25, 62, 63

O

Office of Management and Budget, v, 19

officials, viii, 2, 4, 9, 10, 25, 53, 56, 58, 59, 61, 67, 69, 70, 71, 73, 75, 76, 78, 79, 86, 87
one-dollar coin, 16
operations, 15, 21, 27, 33
opinion polls, 3, 27, 87
opportunities, 32
outreach, 2, 3, 10
overproduction, 7, 12, 37, 40, 42, 44, 45, 46, 47, 64, 80
oversight, 53

P

pain, 25
Philadelphia, 24, 32, 33, 77
pilot study, 71
plants, 24
pleasure, 18, 19
policy, 7, 42, 53, 81
polling, 16
pools, 15
preparation, 28
present value, 56, 82
president, 15, 86
prevention, 15
price index, 86
private sector, vii, 2, 3, 4, 8, 21, 33, 37, 48, 57, 74
production costs, 2, 6, 10, 12, 20, 21, 28, 36, 37, 40, 44, 45, 46, 49, 53, 59, 61, 64, 66, 77, 79, 80
profit, 24, 27
project, 15
public awareness, 10, 81
public debt, 87
public education, 2, 3
public opinion, 9, 10, 11, 70, 71, 87
public policy, 23
public resistance, 3, 10, 57
purchasing power, 10, 12, 61, 86

R

ramp, 25, 65
raw materials, 34, 49, 53, 87
reading, 26
real terms, 80
recommendations, 53, 61
reliability, 13, 23, 53
replacement rate, 65
replacement ratio(s), 6, 36, 37, 38, 39, 40, 47, 48, 53, 65, 66, 80, 82, 83, 84
requirements, 24, 78
resistance, 3, 10, 25, 34, 57
resolution, 87
response, 15, 59, 70, 71
retail, 10, 27, 58, 68, 72
revenue, 14, 17, 32, 33, 87
risk(s), 49, 65, 69, 73, 80
ruble, 63
Russia, 10, 25, 62, 63

S

sampling error, 87
savings, 3, 8, 9, 17, 20, 23, 24, 25, 27, 28, 36, 37, 38, 43, 47, 61, 69, 70
science, 18, 24
scope, 4, 10, 48, 59
Secret Service, viii, 49, 56, 58, 69, 75, 87
Secretary of the Treasury, 49, 59, 61
security, 13, 14, 18, 33, 73
seigniorage, vii, 2, 6, 8, 11, 12, 16, 17, 20, 27, 32, 35, 36, 37, 38, 39, 40, 43, 47, 48, 53, 59, 64, 65, 66, 68, 69, 77, 82, 87
Senate, 35, 37, 57, 58
sensitivity, 49, 66, 74
services, 13
shape, 16
shortage, 15, 47, 65
silver, 33, 61
societal cost, 42, 86
society, 12, 66, 67
solution, 15
Spain, 10, 25, 62, 63

stakeholder outreach, 2, 3, 10
stakeholder views, 1
stakeholders, viii, 3, 8, 9, 10, 17, 18, 21, 34, 42, 56, 57, 58, 72, 73, 75, 76, 82
state, 48, 49
steel, 14, 16, 17, 18, 34
storage, 3, 9, 12, 39, 57, 60, 61, 72
stress, 34
structural changes, 42, 72
structure, 58, 66, 75, 86
substitution, 86
suppliers, 81
surface structure, 14
surplus, 87

T

target, 71
taxes, 20
taxpayers, 23, 25, 31
technical comments, 49, 56, 74
technology(ies), 13, 14, 17, 18, 28, 33
time periods, 75
total product, 80
tracks, 87
trade, 15
training, 72
transactions, 10, 14, 27, 47, 73
transit agencies, 3, 9, 57, 61, 73, 76
transit industry officials, 9
transition period, 6, 11, 12, 39, 40, 44, 45, 46, 56, 64, 66, 72, 79, 81, 83
transport, 3, 57, 60, 72, 73, 76
transportation, 9, 21, 42, 72, 73
Treasury, viii, 2, 4, 7, 24, 26, 27, 28, 37, 38, 42, 48, 49, 52, 55, 56, 58, 59, 61, 74, 75, 80, 85, 86, 88
trial, 34

U

U.S. Department of the Treasury, 63
U.S. economy, 74
underproduction, 80
unforeseen circumstances, 7
United, v, vi, viii, 2, 3, 4, 10, 11, 23, 26, 31, 32, 35, 38, 47, 53, 55, 56, 57, 58, 59, 61, 68, 69, 75, 86
United Kingdom (UK), viii, 2, 3, 4, 10, 11, 25, 47, 53, 55, 56, 57, 58, 62, 63, 65, 66, 69, 71, 74, 75, 80, 87
United States, v, vi, 4, 10, 23, 26, 31, 32, 35, 38, 55, 57, 58, 59, 61, 68, 69, 75, 86
up-front costs, 6, 7, 40, 56

V

validation, 69
variable costs, 79, 81
volatility, 33

W

Washington, 11, 22, 53, 77, 86, 87
wealth, 12
wear, 12, 28, 34
Winnipeg plating facility, 17